Insights
into Liberating
Leadership

How to become a great leader
and create a lasting legacy

Ali Stewart

RETHINK PRESS

First published in Great Britain 2015 by Rethink Press
(www.rethinkpress.com)

Praise for *Insights Into Liberating Leadership*

I have had the privilege to work with Ali and have been struck by her ability to provide insightful contributions whatever the scenario. This book illuminates her thinking in a pragmatic, accessible way. From how and why to use Transactional or Transformational leadership, to deriving lessons from eclectic sources such as Coach Carter, the Karate Kid and even horses. Anyone looking to combine a leadership framework with greater self-awareness should read this book.

ALEX KEAY, INSIGHTS UK GENERAL MANAGER

Ali has truly found her métier. Like all authentic leaders, she lives and breathes this stuff. The crux of her approach – a calm and empathetic style alongside a steely will and desire to succeed is the absolute embodiment of what Liberating Leadership is all about. This book, and the Liberating Leadership programme which it supports, fills a huge gap that I have seen throughout 30+ years of working with leaders in business for a practical, straightforward and robust roadmap for managing and leading others. It should be compulsory reading for all aspiring leaders, existing leaders or those engaged in developing managers and leaders.

MIKE SHEEDY, DIRECTOR, PEAK PERFORMANCE CONSULTANTS

Ali shares with you the proven steps and a methodology for successful transition. She gives insight into how it works and demonstrates through case studies the transition from theory to practice. Ali and the organisations she works with have not won awards by accident. They have won these awards through implementing the steps and applying them in everyday practice.

This is the most complete book I ever read on effective leadership practices. If you embrace and practise these methods and you facilitate them within your own organisation or facilitate and coach them with your clients, not only will you demonstrate authentic leadership, but you will be far more effective with your clients and within the organisations who wish to effect change.

BARBARA EMMANUEL, HR DIRECTOR, SUNSWEPT RESORTS

Great things in business are never done by one person, they're done by a team of people
STEVE JOBS

Thanks to my team, at home and at work, and to everyone who has had a hand in producing this book.

Special thanks to Insights Learning & Development Ltd and Dr Derek Biddle for their trust in me.

CONTENTS

FOREWORD

There are leaders. There are leaders of leaders. Then there are a few who have the gifts and knowledge, the inspiration and mission to empower and enhance the leadership abilities of others. Ali Stewart is such a person. It is fitting that here she is sharing her insights with the wider world.

In today's fast moving, constantly challenging, ever changing world of work, effective leadership at all levels throughout the organisation is an imperative for success. It gets the right things done. But not only that, *Liberating Leadership* builds its own dynamic and momentum for continuing success through motivated, achieving and capable people, successful in their own right.

There are many tomes on leadership. Many claim to have new insights. The claim here is simply that it works. *Liberating Leadership* is a tried and tested process, building skills and giving a step-by-step clear path to follow. It is founded on practical, well proven principles and research. It is award winning. Ali Stewart is its finest practitioner. Read, enjoy and be enthused. For it matters not whether you are new to the subject, are already an experienced effective leader, or are facing challenges at a different level. You will find in these pages how to enhance your abilities further. Bon Voyage.

DR DEREK BIDDLE, AUTHOR OF *LIBERATING LEADERSHIP*

INTRODUCTION

What legacy do you want to leave as a leader?

What do you want your people to say about you?

What do you want them to remember?

What would they say about you now if you were brave enough to ask?

Whether you like it or not, you are leaving a legacy now.

What is your leadership legacy?

Here's the thing: you are almost certainly excellent at what you do. You have had a great idea for a product or service, you have a flair for sales, have spotted a brilliant gap in the market or have risen rapidly inside an organisation because of your quick thinking and drive. You have done well, and guess what? You have now got people around you to support you to achieve even better results.

But I bet you didn't wake up one morning and think, Oh, I'd love to lead a team of people, where can I find them? It kind of happened, and now you have not just yourself to think about, but them too. Managing people is one of the toughest skills to learn in life. I bet you have invested in specialist training in many other areas of your business, but most people have never thought about getting help with people skills. You're way too busy achieving, you haven't had time to indulge in management training.

Unfortunately I have experienced the fallout with my clients. As they push to succeed, sometimes leaving a trail of damaged bodies in their wake, stress is rife. Poor leadership has a negative impact on colleagues, families and health.

For the last eleven years I have been coaching leaders who are seeking more balance, meaning and success in their lives. Having helped over 500 leaders, I've built a reputation for going deep and creating dramatic improvements for them.

Often these leaders believe they are doing their very best for everyone; they work harder and faster than anyone else they know. My success stories come from businesses large and small; in the public or private sectors; in charities; all over the world. What they have in common is that they have all been in danger of burning themselves out, as well as burning those close to them.

The processes and skills in this book truly liberate leaders, their teams and their loved ones. The feedback I get is often deeply moving: "You saved my business"; "You saved my marriage"; "You saved my life!" I am proud of my success stories, and you can be one of them.

Here, then, in this book is the route to liberating your leadership style. It's a dynamic blueprint which helps you as a leader to re-engage your passion:

- your passion for leading your business through your people and valuing them as your greatest resource
- your passion for knowing exactly what action is needed to bring talent on
- your passion for being generous enough to let people grow and proud to let them go with love

This isn't just about leadership, it's about creating the legacy you want to leave.

For the first time ever, here in this book, I've distilled this process into a powerful 8 Point Plan.

Here are the eight points:

1   The Mirror
2   The Crux
3   The Steps
4   The Skills
5   The Secrets
6   The Gear Change
7   The Test
8   The Review

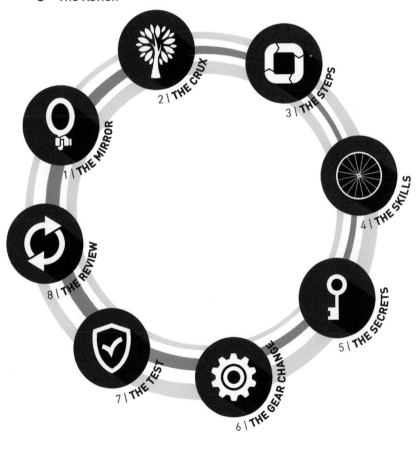

Each chapter guides you through one of these eight points, and they are packed with real leadership stories and examples. I'll also share with you what happens if you don't follow the plan, and how things can go badly wrong – how leaders consistently make life really difficult for themselves and their people.

If you are a business owner, leader or entrepreneur, *Insights into Liberating Leadership* will guide you. I'll help you to see the way to becoming a great leader of people who will make a difference in the world as well as being known for your service or specialism. Whether you struggle with setting your vision, giving feedback, retaining your own sense of assertion and authority, or recruiting and motivating staff, this book will help you, guiding you gently but resolutely through the 8- Point Plan.

I know that you are already passionate about what you do. Your people are your greatest resource: they are the *only* differentiator you have; the only way you can be seen as a market leader; the only way you keep clients coming back again and again.

Discover the eight step process to liberate your leadership legacy.

ALI STEWART

1

THE MIRROR

Leadership starts with you
A colourful take on leadership
How this affects you as leader
Develop your own visible style and legacy
Model the best
Horsing around!

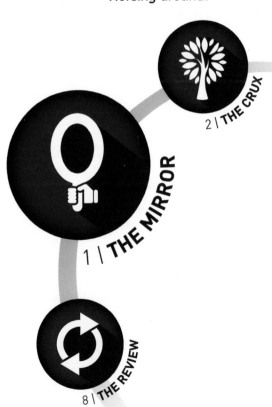

2 | THE CRUX

1 | THE MIRROR

8 | THE REVIEW

THE MIRROR

Leadership starts with you

Great leaders are generally very self-aware – aware of their strengths and limitations – but this is not the case for everyone. Few really appreciate the impact they have on other people, which is why it is important to start with you.

Middle managers often feel as if they are working with their hands tied behind their backs, because they have to manage their own team while also trying to manage upwards. They are not the ones calling the shots, and often have to make sense of changing environments with little direction. They may feel they lack authority and rarely notice just how much of an impact they have on those they manage.

Business owners, leaders and entrepreneurs tend to be so busy running or building their business they focus more on the task than the people. This means they either forget the impact they have, or they may quite

enjoy the dependency and attention of their staff playing to their ego as they build their empire.

On the other hand, team members are very aware of their leader. They notice everything about the leader: when the leader is there and not there; the clothes they wear; the car they drive... they notice every little expression on the leader's face, know when to engage in banter and when not to.

It is for this reason leaders truly need to understand their impact, both through critical self-assessment and through feedback from others. In my experience, leaders are not that great at seeking feedback on their style and behaviour.

An athlete wanting to compete and have any chance of winning has a coach. The relationship between coach and athlete is one of trust, commitment, professionalism and dedication. It is the same for the greatest leaders. They sometimes have a number of coaches to keep them operating at an optimum level, causing them to be lively, liberated leaders.

It can often be demoralising trying to keep going when you don't have access to this kind of executive coaching: which books should you read, which process should you start, and how are you going to fit it in when you are up to your eyes in things?

Insights into Liberating Leadership helps you to start this journey. It guides you through the process, calling on more than twenty-five years of research, testing and validation, so you can quickly develop a thorough grounding in leadership, the like of which you have probably never had. The powerful 8 Point Plan gives you a safe structure to get going.

If you don't take time to look at your leadership style, or are not consistent in the way you operate, you will be leading in a bubble. People will talk behind your back, especially when you're not there. They could even revolt – like they did with brilliant English navigator and explorer, Captain William Bligh, whose major flaw was a lack of consistency. This was so bad his crew staged the well-known Mutiny on the Bounty.

> *There were a number of things about him that were causing a measure of uneasiness – the uncertain nature of his moodiness, the way he would nag, nag, nag away on some failure, real or supposed, large or small one day, then ignore some serious piece of mismanagement the next day. There wasn't any consistency about the man.*
>
> **CAPTAIN BLIGH AND MR CHRISTIAN BY RICHARD HOUGH**

You wouldn't want a mutiny on your Bounty, and generally when you think of somebody who doesn't have consistency, you think, Can I trust them? Can I depend on them to deliver? What's their game? It can be a little unnerving. So, developing your own self-awareness is critical – consistency is a vital part of this.

This is why we start here, at point one of the plan, where we *hold up the mirror*, giving you the means to take a good look at *you*.

If you miss out this point and jump straight to step two or three, it's likely that you'll experience a high turnover of staff, you'll become so disgruntled you leave, or your best team members will leave and you will wonder why running a business is so incredibly difficult.

A colourful take on leadership

With any new client, I start by getting the leader and their team to complete an online evaluator, giving them access to the most beautiful, accurate psychometric tool of its kind. It's called *Insights Discovery®*.

The model is highly memorable and user-friendly, and has an instant and wonderful impact on people, producing feedback like this:

I found my Insights Discovery profile fascinating and enjoyable to read, I kept laughing as I read things about myself. It seems disarmingly accurate!

I must confess to being amazed by the accuracy and insight of the Insights Discovery profile. I agree with the areas flagged up as development points and will definitely try to strengthen these. (Well, some at least!)

I really enjoyed receiving my feedback. It's like finally being able to view yourself from another's perspective.

Some of the detail is scarily accurate. There's the odd detail I'm less sure about, but, for the most part it's pretty spot on and fascinating, if a little disconcerting!

Based firmly on the pioneering personality profiling work of the renowned psychologist Dr Carl G Jung, the *Insights Discovery®* model has transformed thousands of lives.

Since ancient times, philosophers have identified four broad types of personality. Carl Jung further developed this idea in the twentieth century. He suggested that all four personality types or energies are present in all of us, and the different balances between them are what make us unique.

The Insights Discovery® personal profile measures those balances in a disarmingly powerful way, leading to amazing performance breakthroughs. Every page in the profile is helpful, and the pointers on the *Suggestions for Development* page can be worked into a personal improvement plan.

Although I am accredited to use a number of psychometric tools, in 2003 when I attended the four day accreditation programme to be a Licensed Practitioner with Insights, it blew my mind. Such was the dramatic impact it had on me, it inspired me to set up my own business, which I did in 2004 – and I haven't looked back!

Now, when we deliver the Liberating Leadership programme, we first take the leader and team members – which could be the senior leadership team – through the Insights Discovery® model. They have an individual profile as well as a view of the team as a whole, which is presented as a colourful visual picture which everyone can see. We have a fun interactive day based on this amazing colour model, and it becomes the language for communication in the organisation or department. I can't get started with leadership skill building until every leader has an Insights Discovery® personal profile. It is possible to use another profiling tool, but this is definitely the best one I've come across. I love the fact that at its most simple it has just four colour energies, so even children can understand it (it has helped my three children so much over the years), and you can then go as deep as you like. The tool itself is being constantly developed.

The basic four Insights Discovery colour energies are:

- Cool Blue
- Fiery Red
- Sunshine Yellow
- Earth Green

The profile you receive is a powerful development tool, giving you information on your own perceived strengths, weaknesses, value to the team, communication style, blind spots, how to deal with your opposite type and suggestions for development. It also shows you how much of each colour energy you use. It is an incredibly personal tool – your profile will be unique to you – and a market leader.

Positive use of the Insights Discovery colour energies can be seen like this:

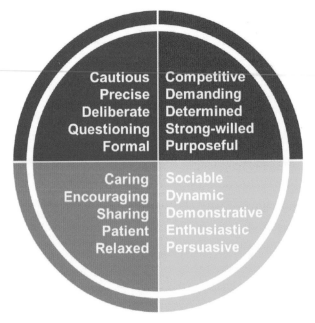

And if you overuse any of these strengths, then they could be seen more like this:

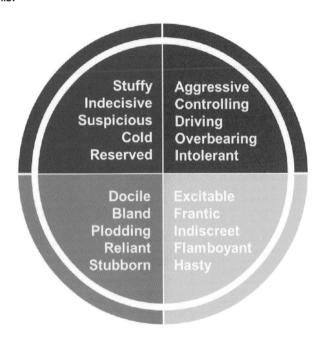

The overused preferences are what you can display under pressure, or when you're really relaxed with people and don't have to be on your best behaviour with them.

On the basis we all possess all four colour energies, the model identifies how much of each colour energy you use and to what intensity. Mostly we have a preference for one or two colours more than the others.

From the simple statements in the colour energy graphics, you can quickly assess the colour energies to which you are more drawn and in

Reference to Insights Discovery® and the colour energy graphics are by kind permission of Insights Learning & Development Ltd what order you might put them. As we have all four colour energies in us, we may access them at different times, and with age and experience we learn how to access them better. But be very wary of saying you use all four colours equally, because this is incredibly rare.

- What order would you put them in?
- What impact does this have?
- Thinking about the people you work with, what might their preference be?
- What action do you need to take as a result of this?

When you complete the Insights Discovery® online evaluator which produces your profile, from your responses the software will position you carefully in one of the four quadrants, and it will show you how easily you can access the other three.

Knowing which colour preference you lead with and which comes second is fundamental. For instance, if I lead with competitive, demanding, slightly intolerant Fiery Red energy and my second preference is Sunshine Yellow, this brings with it a sociable, dynamic, excitable quality. Whereas, if Cool Blue is my second preference there would be more precision, caution and suspicion.

Understanding your attitude to your opposite type, or to anyone with a similar colour preference, is key. Looking at the colourful Insights Discovery energy diagrams, you will see that Fiery Red and Earth Green are opposite, Cool Blue and Sunshine Yellow are opposite.

This means if you lead with Earth Green energy, you may consider those high in Fiery Red energy as aggressive rather than assertive, or even downright rude and abrasive. Those leading with Fiery Red energy often observe those high in Earth Green energy as more docile and slow, stubborn and difficult to read.

Those leading with Sunshine Yellow energy can experience people high in Cool Blue energy as more stuffy, cold and somewhat distant. If you are high in Cool Blue energy, you may see those high in Sunshine Yellow as more flappy, frantic and overly dramatic.

> *If one does not understand a person, one tends to regard him as a fool.*
>
> **DR CARL G JUNG**

The greatest leaders need to access all four quadrants at different times, so understanding where you are and how easy this is for you is crucial. When we move into Liberating Leadership, you will see how the colour preferences flow through the 4 Step Leadership Process. Much of my time is spent coaching and developing leaders to reach a greater depth of understanding and balance.

How this affects you as leader

All of this has obvious implications on the way you are likely both to view and treat others, along with the culture of the organisation you are in or team you might create.

Understanding yourself with the help of a tool like the Insights Discovery® model enables you to see clearly what kind of leader you are and the kind of impact you might have.

Two leaders of a team with whom I've been working recently demonstrate the differences starkly. One leads with sociable, flexible Sunshine Yellow energy and wants everyone in the team to be like a big, happy family: free to challenge and ask questions; free to make mistakes and be supported. The other leads with assertive, demanding Fiery Red energy and, although he wants the team members to be happy, he wants to see high performance right now. He wants them to get on and get the job done, and be as motivated to achieve as he is. He can't abide laziness or under performance, and his displeasure shows on his face.

Team members and others naturally go to the one who leads with Sunshine Yellow energy to ask questions. They feel safe as the leader is more open and friendly. The downside (for the leader) is team members know they can get away with murder, in a manner of speaking. The team members fear the other leader as he is more apt to shoot from the hip, especially when he's annoyed.

Now that these two leaders have been through the programme and understand the Liberating Leadership approach, they are achieving altogether different results. Team members are behaving properly, stepping up to the mark, rising to the challenge and appreciating much clearer direction.

Every advance, every conceptual achievement of mankind has been connected with an advance in self-awareness.

DR CARL G JUNG

Develop Your Own Visible Style and Legacy

- What kind of a leader are you?
- What kind of a leader do you want to be?
- What do you want to be known for?
- What do you want people to say about you when you leave?

These are powerful questions to ask yourself, as your responses will show you the areas you need to develop if you are not there yet. The Insights Discovery® personal profile will help you find the answers if you are not sure. You start with a personal profile and can then go as deep as you like; there is now a *Deeper Discovery* model which can help you develop even greater self-awareness in an irresistibly powerful way. You then start to lead your life with meaning, rather than leave it to fate or a more empty drive to succeed.

Making your style really visible to people and making it clear what you stand for is essential. As the saying goes, "If you don't stand for something, you'll fall for anything." If you are definite about what you believe, people can line up behind you.

They will:

- come and work for you because they want to, not because they have to
- work with their blood, sweat and tears, not just for money
- believe in you and give you their all, and not merely treat you as their employer

Model the best

A good way to develop your style is to model yourself on others who are doing this well. Which leaders capture your imagination and who do you want to be like? Are you a Bill Gates or Richard Branson; Mahatma Ghandi or Nelson Mandela; Karen Brady or Oprah Winfrey; Sheryl Sandberg or Anita Roddick? It would be worth stopping right now to decide how you want to be seen.

If you want to be a great, high-performing leader, then *Liberating Leadership* by Dr Derek Biddle gives you the perfect way to model yourself on the best. Derek has studied more than 500 leaders, who aren't necessarily famous or people you know, but they have bubbled to the top in organisations you do know. Organisations like Gillette and Vodafone, what was Friends Provident (now Friends Life), Severn Trent Water, the Foreign and Commonwealth Office, and many smaller companies up and down the UK.

We will be talking a lot more about *Liberating Leadership* in the chapters to come. There are four self-assessment tools which are an integral part of the programme. These naturally follow on from your Insights Discovery® profile, and help to build your competence as an inspirational leader of people.

With personality there is no right or wrong; each person is unique. The Insights Discovery® personal profile gives you a chance to reflect on your personal style, and shows you how to adapt to get a better result. With leadership, there *is* a right and wrong. For instance, there are some skills you need at the beginning of the leadership process which you don't need at the end, and vice versa. If you get these skills in the wrong order, things will not go quite the way you want. This will leave you feeling that managing people is difficult and you would prefer just to get on with your own thing.

Horsing around!

Before we move onto the next chapter, and at the risk of sounding like a crazy woman, can I talk to you about horses for a moment? This is incredibly relevant to holding up the mirror, because horses offer another great way of 'seeing' yourself.

I've been practising tapping into all four colour energies with horses. They do it so easily and they are brilliant teachers. Sometimes I take groups of leaders and practitioners out to work with horses, especially if they are struggling to establish for themselves the skills of high performing leaders.

If you are walking along leading a horse with a rope, the only way you can make it walk between two long poles on the ground is by engaging sufficient Fiery Red assertive energy. If you aren't determined enough, it will step outside the poles. If you come to long poles lying sideways across your path, and you need the horse to step neatly between the poles with each hoof, by quietly engaging your Cool Blue energy you can do this with the precision needed. Failure to engage this type of energy would result in the horse stepping right across the poles, particularly with its hind legs.

You then engage your nurturing Earth Green energy and encourage the horse to be still with you – you know you've achieved success if the horse puts its head down. Sometimes the connection between leader and horse is so profound it has moved people to tears.

Then you engage your happy Sunshine Yellow energy and encourage the horse to dance with you. And I tell you what: if you can make half a ton of horse dance round an arena in time with your lead, you know with absolute clarity that you can lead your people.

Having overcome my fear of horses by working with them in this way, I have observed at least five things that a horse can teach us about leadership. I don't know if you have ever really looked at a horse and spoken to it, but if you do (and people who do will know exactly what I mean) you then develop a deep sense of stillness and connection, and words are no longer necessary.

1   Horses see things at a level we only go to occasionally, sometimes never. Developing a connection like this without ever seeking to ride the animal is amazing. Imagine if you could connect with your people at this level and what that might mean

for you as a leader. You will understand in the moment what each person needs.

2   Horses can tell you things about you which people either don't see or don't want to tell you — perhaps because you wouldn't want to listen or acknowledge if they did. Being a leader can be a lonely existence, with people always bowing down to your perceived superior knowledge or energy. Imagine how much more effective you could be with some really challenging feedback. A horse doesn't hold back; if it doesn't think you are authentic, it will simply turn round and show you its rump. This happened to one leader when he was trying to encourage the horse to go with him without first connecting with the horse. He laughed as the penny dropped, and said, 'Oh boy, my staff have been telling me for years I don't listen, and I didn't believe them. Now I'm getting the message loud and clear!'

3   Horses are wonderful teachers, and will have infinite patience as you learn to see what they can see in you. Bearing in mind we only use a fraction of our total capacity, imagine learning things about you that would transform your leadership competence and style.

4   Horses help you develop clarity and focus, purpose and intention, grace and kindness, and overcome your fears, even a fear of horses. This really helps you to develop your visibility of style and approach, and be the leader you want to be; the leader you were born to be.

5   Imagine magnetically attracting what you desire. Imagine without speaking you ask a horse to follow you – and it does.

When this happens, you begin to experience a new level of connection with others, which you can easily transfer to your interactions with your team with dramatic results.

In chapter 6 we'll hear a beautiful story from one of the Liberating Leadership practitioners, Sally Foan, about how she used this approach to gain the trust of her new, big, previously badly beaten horse.

You'll have got the message now that there are different ways for you to take a long, hard look at yourself. Insights Discovery® is magically powerful, modelling other leaders is an excellent discipline, and if you prefer something bigger and even more dramatic...you know what to do.

Insights Discovery and Insights Learning Systems were originated by Andi and Andy Lothian

Reference to Insights Discovery® and the colour energy graphics are by kind permission of Insights Learning & Development Ltd

2

THE CRUX

Setting the ground rules
The Critical Mindset – getting the balance right
So how do you know if you've got it?
Six things you need to know
Cool visioning exercise

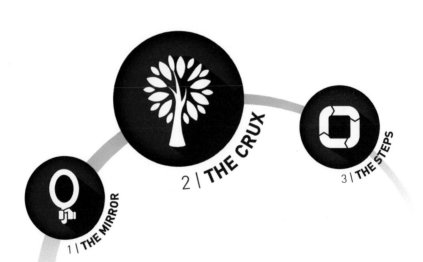

1 | THE MIRROR

2 | THE CRUX

3 | THE STEPS

THE CRUX

The crux of anything is the nub, the root, the central piece on which everything is built, and without which everything will collapse. This gives you a sense of the importance of this second point in the 8 Point Plan. It is the underpinning ethos, shared by the highest performing leaders, which formed the basis of the research for Dr Derek Biddle's acclaimed Liberating Leadership programme, for which Ali Stewart & Co is the accrediting body. *Liberating Leadership* is the book for you to read next, and I will give you a flavour of it here.

Setting the ground rules

The crux of being a high performing leader has a couple of elements. First, it is vital for leaders to set their *vision* and *ground rules* around behaviour.

Although people often turn up and do a job in return for money without appreciating or even caring why they are there, the way leaders build passion and commitment in their people is to share their big vision. The purpose of *Insights into Liberating Leadership* isn't to tell you how to do this because I have so many other things to share with you, but setting your vision is very important, as you will see, so I will give you a few pointers.

At the end of this chapter you will find a cool visioning exercise to help you dream your way to success and loosen up your mind. If you are ready to stand up, shake your limbs and expand your mind, then why not go ahead and do it right now.

You can model yourself on famous people who have had big visions in the past. For instance you can pop onto YouTube and watch Simon Sinek's TED talk, *The Golden Circle*, in which he says, 'People don't buy what you do, they buy *why* you do it.' Also read his book, *Start with the Why.* He talks about:

- Martin Luther King's 'I Have a Dream' speech. That didn't just happen; Dr King worked on that speech for years, tried it out hundreds of times on smaller groups of people, but he had the vision and knew what he wanted to achieve, and he kept saying it until he found the right time and the right place for a movement to start.

- Steve Jobs of Apple saying, 'Everything we do we believe in challenging the status quo, we believe in thinking differently'. Apple also happen to make great computers.

- And Nike, 'Inspiration and innovation for every athlete in the world', just happen to make great running shoes.

Your vision sets out your purpose: why you are here, which comes from the heart. Do whatever work you need to do to make this really clear. Even if you are the leader of a department in a massive organisation, you can still have a very clear vision about the way you want your team to operate. What value do you want to add as leader of this team? In Chapter 5 I'll be sharing what coach Ken Carter thought about being leader of a high school basketball team. He had a big vision –

what some call a BHAG: Big Hairy Audacious Goal. He could just have turned up quietly and coached the team in the skills of basketball, but he wanted to make a difference to the boys' lives. He wanted them to have a chance of graduating, and not succumb to the gun crime and drugs the area was known for.

So what is your big vision for your team right now?

What difference are you going to make to your organisation?

What footprint are you going to leave in the sand?

Ground rules are needed to guide people in how to achieve your vision: the kind of behaviour that will be allowed, the kind that is expected, and what will happen if a person can't work within these parameters. For instance, you might be happy with flexible working, but would not want this to be abused. There might be rules around respect and the way you speak with each other. The rules could be around the dress code for operating in this team or how you treat clients. Becoming very clear about what you will allow and then sharing that with the team is vital.

Although setting out your *vision* and *ground rules* up front is crucial, it's a principle many leaders fail to do clearly enough. Imagine you are the pilot of a plane. You do your preparation before you take off, know the destination, have your charts showing how you're going to get there, check current and future weather conditions, check equipment, fuel and team. In your mind you mentally fly the route to spot things that might go wrong, and only when you have done all your checks are you cleared for take-off. However, we observed in the research that only the high performing leaders had this kind of rigour in their planning. If you haven't done your planning, it would be a good idea to stop and do it right now.

When you've set your *vision* and established the *ground rules*, it will make the rest of the leadership process so much easier in terms of being able to give strong, clear feedback and keeping your team motivated and engaged. You'll be halfway cleared for take-off, and you'll be ready for the second part of The Crux, which is sorting out your mindset. This is the tricky bit, and we'll look at it next so that you can be cleared for take-off and get going.

The Critical Mindset – getting the balance right

Having set your *vision* and *ground rules*, the second vital element of The Crux is to do with your *mindset* as leader.

Two things tend to happen for leaders. See which camp you fall in:

1   You try to be everyone's friend and end up doing all the work yourself

2 You push people like you do yourself and get frustrated with them when they can't keep up

Every leader is guilty of doing too much of one or the other. In the first instance you are giving too much support, and in the second instance too much challenge.

This critical mindset is to operate with *High Challenge and High Support*. And getting the perfect balance of these two extremes is the sweet spot for leaders. Your personality type will tend to dictate which one you use more; aligning them in powerful and equal combination is absolutely key.

Another way of looking at this is through the words of a song: '...you gotta be cruel to be kind, in the right measure'. If you get it wrong, you'll know about it.

As a leader, being too kind suggests you might be prone to smothering. It means you are doing too much for the other person, finishing off a job rather than showing them how to do it. You might hold back from commenting on mistakes and just correct things yourself. You might work late to finish the work, allowing your people to go early. Then you start resenting them.

This state is not healthy for you or anyone else. It keeps you pinned to completing day to day tasks with never enough time to be strategic or do your marketing, and your people aren't able to develop, which isn't ideal, even though they may be happy in this state. They're happy because you, their leader, do everything for them: you watch their back; you are kind, and they are rarely in trouble because you tend to take the blame for anything going wrong.

Being too cruel, on other hand, is extremely unkind. Here the leader is constantly criticising what their people are doing. They may have a 'hire and fire' mentality. They may set extreme goals which are impossible for anyone to achieve, which can be very demotivating. Instead of discussing how to do things, they give commands. And rather than having an interest in developing people, these leaders expect people to know what to do and get on with it, or else they'll be out the door.

The mindset of High Challenge and High Support is the *golden thread* which weaves through the leader's journey, supporting the other elements in the 8 Point Plan. We will keep referring to it as we go along, because it's so very important. Without this golden thread, sooner or later the edges become frayed and things will disintegrate – your company, your team, and you.

Striking the balance right is critical, but not always easy to do until you start paying attention to it.

> *It is the combination of Challenge and Support – the both/and principle – which really matters.*
>
> **DR DEREK BIDDLE**

So how do you know if you've got it?

The aim is to have High Challenge and High Support in powerful and equal combination. Too much of one or the other will lead to a state where people are not achieving their full potential. The team falls short of being high performing when you as leader are not pushing people to be the best they can. Too much challenge would mean you are simply pushing them; too much support means you are not pushing them at all.

Let's have look at the options and you can decide what you are like.

1   High Challenge/High Support: If a leader operates with a perfect balance of High Challenge and High Support, they will be rewarded with consistent high achievement and development from their people. The team will have a good reputation. Some people will move on when they've reached their peak, and others will be keen to join the team because of this reputation.

2   High Challenge/Low Support: Too much challenge will be stressful for everybody. High achievement will at best be random and inconsistent – the stakes are high, and so are tempers. Typically in this environment there is a rapid turnover of staff, as it's all about results and not about the people – if you can't stand the heat, get out of the kitchen!

3   High Support/Low Challenge: Too much support is often more comfortable for staff, but issues are not dealt with directly, and people are never challenged to improve constantly. This leads to moderate achievement, and under-achievers are pushed sideways but never out. We all know organisations like this. People tend to be very loyal because it's typically a nice place to work, but people aren't pressed to achieve excellence.

4   Low Challenge/Low Support: Low Challenge and Low Support leads to apathy. It really doesn't matter whether anybody achieves or not – in which case you may as well pack up and go home. This is a very unhealthy place to be, and if you've ever found yourself here, you know you need to find a new job or start out on your own as quickly as possible.

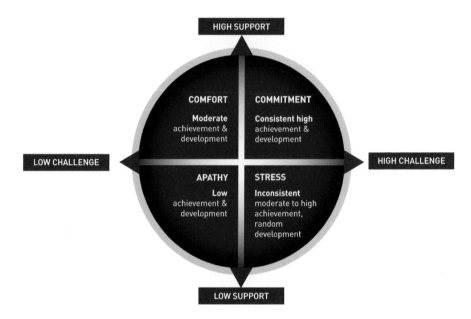

From the descriptions, you are likely to be able to assess where you or your organisation is right now, and maybe where it has been and where it's heading. But how do you get the balance right? How do you get challenge and support in powerful and equal combination, and why generally are leaders not very good at it?

One of the questionnaires in the Liberating Leadership programme allows you to assess yourself on the High Challenge/High Support balance, which provides a very useful health check. There is a 360 element available so you can gather feedback from those above you, below you, beside you, your suppliers, your clients — a range of people who can comment on your style from their perspective. Gathering feedback in this way enables you to have some great conversations with the people giving the feedback, which really helps your development as a powerful leader of people.

There is a guiding framework to make sure the elements making up The Crux are used ethically to help people rather than manipulate them unkindly. To help you understand there are six things you need to know, which we'll look at next.

Six things you need to know

The six things are chunked in pairs for ease of reference.

Research Findings

1   'The highest performing leaders were similar and consistent in what they did.' (Dr Derek Biddle) So, irrespective of the type of company, whether public or private sector, big or little, the highest performing leaders were doing the same thing – which not only made it easier to capture what they were doing, it makes it very easy for others to model.

2   'They were not "charismatic heroes" but ordinary people who had discovered a particular way of working.' (Dr Derek Biddle) This means anyone can learn to be a high performing leader. You don't need any special qualifications, you just need to get into the mindset and learn the way of working.

The Concepts

3   People generally respond better to praise rather than criticism, although criticism is far better than being ignored. So reinforcing good behaviour and catching people doing something right on

a day by day basis is critical. This may seem obvious, but so often we throw a fit when things go wrong, while taking the good stuff for granted.

4   Have a vision of people performing at their very best, which is really hard to do if people are consistently under-achieving, but if you expect high performance you are far more likely to get it. Put people down in your mind and that's exactly where they'll stay. I'll share with you a little story about this in a minute to explain the crucial impact this can have.

The Attitudes

5   The first attitude you need is one of *Positive Regard*. This means having respect for someone as an individual and a positive belief in them as a person. Irrespective of the behaviour they are displaying, you see the good in them and view them as a decent human being.

6   The second attitude is *Genuineness*, where you are able to express your own feelings and tell the truth about your reactions to a person's behaviour. It means being direct, open and honest with this person, not shying away from difficult conversations.

If you take the Attitudes – Positive Regard and Genuineness – at a superficial level they may seem like common sense. Surely everyone has them. However, in my experience it tends to go with colour energy, linking back to your Insights Discovery® preferences. For instance, if you are high in Earth Green nurturing energy, you may connect more with Positive Regard and generally treat people kindly, giving them the benefit of the doubt. What you may struggle with is Genuineness, because you don't like conflict so you are more likely to shy away from being frank and open with someone if their behaviour has upset you. You withdraw and explain it away somehow, opting for an easy life rather than having to confront the individual.

Those with higher Fiery Red assertive energy tend to be happier with Genuineness – they are very able to tell another person what they think of their behaviour in the moment. What they really need to watch is Positive Regard, because what is likely to be expressed by their face and tone is 'You imbecile'.

As Positive Regard and Genuineness form the bedrock for you operating with High Challenge/High Support, you have to be very honest with yourself in assessing how well you deal with these. So it is when we talk about High Challenge and High Support – you need to check you are in the right mindset to think like this. When you do, you will achieve astonishing results. It will certainly help you to understand the process of leadership, which is clearly defined, distinct and understandable, in the next chapter.

Going back to one of the concepts – the ability to visualise people performing at their very best, even when they are currently not operating at this level – I promised to share a story.

This story concerns my older son, Sam, who is intensely bright, very tempestuous and quick to anger with his 99% Fiery Red energy. His second energy is Cool Blue. This means he is action-oriented with a desperate need for information to help him process and analyse things in his mind. And he needs the information now, and woe betide anyone if he doesn't get it.

While at a very good all boys secondary school, Sam was constantly at odds with the teachers. He was very unruly, didn't hand in his homework because he thought the task was stupid, and had so many after school detentions he couldn't fit any more in his diary. He was constantly getting into scraps with other boys because of his temper; he was just as difficult at home, although at least he had respect for his dad and me, but not so for the teachers. We were being called into school by the Head of Year to talk about his appalling behaviour nearly every week. If there was trouble anywhere in school, Sam was at the root of it.

Sam's dreadful behaviour was the subject of much discussion between Neil, my husband, and me. We were always talking about the bad things Sam was doing: *if only he would keep his mouth shut and not argue with teachers; if only he would do his homework; if only he'd keep his fists to himself; if only he didn't keep getting detention...* – we were in a negative downward spiral of despair about him. When I realised what we were doing I stopped, got an exercise book and put it by my bed. Each night before going to sleep, I wrote down all the good things about Sam. I tried to spot different things every day – *he's a great conversationalist; he is really good with Rory, his little brother; he will push the Hoover round if I ask him (what fifteen-year-old boy would do that?); he'll willingly come with me to visit his grandparents...*

The impact this had was phenomenal. It changed my behaviour towards him. Instead of waking up in the morning, seeing Sam and saying, 'Try and keep your nose clean and out of other people's business today' or 'Keep your mouth shut if you know what's good for you', I would give him a hug and say, 'Sam, I love you. I really hope you have a good day today.' Can you imagine the difference this made to him walking out the door, rather than going out with the usual admonitions?

His behaviour slowly began to change, and I'll tell you more about Sam (who I call my teacher) as we go through. He has definitely taught me to be a better leader.

Cool Visioning Exercise

If you can dream it, you can do it

WALT DISNEY

This is an exercise you can try at home; it busts through your limiting beliefs. Anyone can do it. Are you ready to give it a go? It's probably best if you read the instructions first, then try it for yourself.

You need to stand in a clear space and make sure you can swing your arms round without them bashing into anything.

- Stand up straight with your feet slightly apart, centred comfortably beneath your shoulders, arms by your side.
- Throughout the exercise, keep your feet firmly on the floor – they need to stay perfectly still.
- Now raise your right arm as if you are pointing to something straight ahead of you – your arm should be at a right angle to your body.
- Keeping your feet in place, gently move your arm round to the right and see how far round the room you can comfortably point – can you go a bit further? – and mentally mark the place on the wall.

- Bring your arm back round and drop it down by your side.
- Keeping your feet in place, close your eyes. Without physically doing anything, imagine you are raising your right arm out in front of you and slowly moving it round to the right...you easily pass your first and second points and it feels really fluid, really easy. Then imagine you are bringing your arm back round and dropping it down by your side
- One more time, keeping your eyes closed and your feet still, repeat the previous point. You beat your first, second and third points; it feels so easy, everything is so fluid and free. Then imagine you are bringing your arm back round again and dropping it down by your side.
- Now open your eyes. This time really raise your right arm, move it gently round to the right... Feel the difference!

OK, now it's your turn. Clear your mind, relax and give it a go.

Typically, if I do this with a room full of people, there are oohs and aahs as people feel their bodies releasing and allowing their arm to go much further, without anything hurting. In fact, one person shared with me that his right shoulder had been stiff previously, and now it felt much better.

I would absolutely love to hear how you get on!

If we did all the things we are capable of, we would literally astound ourselves.

THOMAS A EDISON

3

THE STEPS

The Clear 4 Step Process
Drive your way to success
A 'rum' case study
How to lead yourself through the Steps

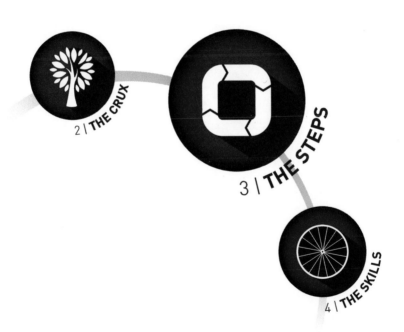

2 | THE CRUX

3 | THE STEPS

4 | THE SKILLS

THE STEPS

This chapter will enable leaders to feel a great sense of relief. Rather than constantly working things out by trial and error when it comes to managing and leading people, there is a clear process to follow. All it needs is a commitment to start at the beginning and see it through to the end.

When we talk about personality, there is no right or wrong. You are a fabulous, unique individual. When it comes to leadership, however, there is a right way to lead, and if you do things in the right order it will help any issues you have as a leader to melt away.

Instead of being ground down by teams and departments working in silos, people squabbling, coming in with all their problems, not living up to expectations, and you getting caught up in the emotion of it all, you can relax. With this process you will know exactly what you are going to do to fix unwanted behaviours, every step of the way. No longer will people baffle you. You are going to get skilled at diagnosing the root cause of their behaviour and have a plan for dealing with it.

As a leader, you *can* become more detached emotionally so that you remain objective, while at the same time having an even better relationship with your people.

Interestingly, people don't leave organisations, they leave because of their leader. By making your people more important than anything, you'll find they do the work needed and support you, releasing you to do the things you are good at and should be doing.

The Clear 4 Step Process

In our Liberating Leadership programme, which is a result of Dr Derek Biddle's critical look at both leaders of our time and a good deal of the existing management theory, this very clear process is perfectly described. I'm just going to give you a flavour of it here to help you see how you can drive your way to success.

There is nothing new about four step processes for leaders. They have been documented over time by countless management gurus. One such process is Hersey and Blanchard's *Situational Leadership* model – Telling, Selling, Participating, Delegating. However, there are three things which set our 4 Step Process apart from all the rest:

1   *It is underpinned by The Crux.*

It doesn't stand alone. The elements making up The Crux really support the process through:

- having a clear vision and setting the ground rules
- operating with a mindset of High Challenge/High Support, used in powerful and equal combination
- having high expectations – constantly holding in your mind a vision of each member of your team performing excellently
- catching people doing something right so you are consistently reinforcing the behaviours needed to achieve your goals and vision
- acting with Positive Regard and Genuineness

These elements are so crucial, and generally not taught in other models. I remember in the early days when I delivered the Liberating Leadership accreditation programme on my own for the very first time (previously I had had the support and guidance of Derek), a very experienced leadership coach stopped me after a while. Looking serious, he put his elbows on the table in front of him, leaned forward and said in a gruff voice, 'Do you mean to tell me we can't become Liberating Leadership practitioners unless we get this central mindset?'

I pondered the question for just a moment, then looked up and said, 'Yes. If you don't agree with this, we can't go on. We'll shake hands and call it a day, this is not the programme for you.'

I held my breath, wishing Derek was there to support me... and the coach said, 'Good. I wanted to know how important this was. Now I understand it is of fundamental importance. I like that, it's powerful.'

2 *The way it's used.*

The highest performing leaders in the research excelled because they rigorously used the process, purposefully going through it with every person and using all four steps well.

3 *The fifteen high performing leader skills.*

There are fifteen generic leadership skills which flow through the process, some of which are rarely taught. I can't wait to share them with you – the secrets are revealed in Chapter 5.

What most leaders do is to dabble with the process and do the steps they like doing, rather than selecting the most appropriate step for the situation. It goes with personality type, which is another reason why it is always best to start by holding up the mirror so leaders have a better understanding of their own attitudes towards the Process, and understand why they find some parts more difficult.

Now you need to know what the four steps are. Each step has a name to describe what goes on during that stage as a guide for leaders to know their primary focus in each step.

We start at the bottom with Step 1 – Visioning.

Enabling

Developing

Mobilising

Visioning

We started setting your vision with The Crux to get you thinking about it. To know where you are going is crucial, otherwise your company or department will be like a rudderless ship, easily blown off course. You need to know the purpose of your team – *why* you are here – and then share it so everyone in the team knows what they are working towards. I know I've mentioned it before, but do watch Simon Sinek's TED talk *How Great Leaders Inspire Action*. This will really help you to understand the *why* part.

You will appreciate this first step takes a lot of your time as leader. You need to be visible, certain about your own style (which your Insights Discovery® profile helps you with), and get things going. Then once everyone is clear about the vision and you have an accurate assessment of the situation, you need to move into action.

This is where you click into Step 2 – Mobilising.

The skills needed to get people doing what needs to be done in the way you want it done are described in more detail later. You just need to know that again this step takes a lot of your time. You need to be around to spot when things are being done well and when they are not.

You need, and get at this stage, a dynamic method for diagnosing poor performance.

This is such a powerful tool for leaders, many clients ask me if they can just buy this diagnostic flowchart, which we call the Performance Navigator. It makes so much sense to them. It is incredibly robust, fits with their other systems, such as their disciplinary and grievance procedures, and stands up to scrutiny if faced with a tribunal.

The most under-emphasised skill happens in this Mobilising stage: the art of *explicitness*. This is the ability to explain very clearly what behaviour will be regarded by you as good, and what behaviour will be deemed to be unacceptable in the circumstances. Some leaders will do the first part and say what they want, most leaders don't do the latter part.

The ability to be explicit works in every walk of life, not just for traditional leaders. This is a secret which we will unpick in Chapter 5, and is one of the most vital and useful parts of your leadership toolkit.

In this Mobilising stage you are no longer planning ahead. The vision has been set, and you have to be there to respond moment by moment as things happen. You are paying attention to everything that goes on. Your actions must be clear, as there can be disastrous consequences if you don't get things right at this stage and bad habits form.

For instance, if you have set the ground rules but you don't notice whether people are adhering to them or comment on their behaviour, the team will be watching to see what happens. If you take no action, they will assume you are not serious and won't respect the ground rules. You may as well not have bothered.

Next is Step 3 – Developing

As you move into Step 3, you can take a more hands-off approach. Your team members are now consistently doing things right and begin to have some input into how things are done. You've developed their level of skill and will to do things, and you can see their own internal motivation to do the job has kicked in. As the leader you can afford to watch more from a distance, so this stage is not nearly so time-intensive for you.

I share more about this step in the following section, and also in Chapter 6 when we take a more careful look at when to move through the steps. You will then really appreciate the difference in style needed at this stage of the process.

Finally, Step 4 – Enabling.

If you reach this stage you're doing really well, because most leaders don't. This is one of the things that set the high performing leaders apart in the research: they were very good at moving their team members to this stage. It's the stage of high capability and competence. Your team members can do things better than you. The student becomes the master and doesn't need you interfering in what they're doing – they now own the task.

At the moment, I'm just giving you an overview of this very important step. It is going to need your time and attention to use it well and get it right. It will seem weird, because you really don't have to do too much in terms of managing people. You are at what we call the Transformational Leadership stage – you are spotting new opportunities and providing the inspiration for your team to keep going on a journey of continuous improvement.

By moving smoothly through the 4 Step Process you can literally...

Drive your way to success

Imagine you are driving a car – I mean a basic kind of car with just four manual gears. Moving through the gears of the car is exactly what moving through the 4 Step Process is like. If you don't drive, then I'm sure you'll connect with the analogy anyway because you're bound to have at least been in a car. We'll talk about yachts and flight plans later in the book if that's more your thing.

Way back when I learnt to drive, I was lucky enough to be given a little old Hillman Imp by my mum and dad for my seventeenth birthday. It had a spindly gear stick, four sweet gears and reverse; it was painted turquoise and it had character. It was called Eddie. My dad taught me to drive in Eddie; I didn't have any formal driving lessons and passed my test first time.

What my dad said, amongst other things, was 'Listen to your engine, you'll hear when to change gear' and 'Keep an eye on your instrument panel to check your speed and for any warning lights'.

Thanks, Dad!

This was sound advice, which also works really well for leaders to navigate their way through the 4 Step Process:

The very best gear for pulling away from the kerb is first gear (Visioning). If you try and start in second gear your engine will be a bit sluggish; starting in third gear could cause your engine to chug, choke and stall, possibly causing some damage; and you won't get very far if you try and pull away in fourth gear.

- Before you start, you generally know where you're going and have assessed the weather conditions. Hopefully you've got a shovel, blanket and flask when the outlook is cold and snowy, in case you get stuck. You make sure your wipers are working, your windscreen washer container is topped up and you check your tyres.

- To keep the engine nicely lubricated and keep the car going, you top up with oil and fuel as needed.

- You visualise how you are going to get to your destination by planning your route, making sure you've had enough sleep and allowing for plenty of pit stops along the way – in an ideal world!

- For your car to stay fit for purpose and to iron out any mechanical issues that arise, you know you need to get it regularly serviced, and definitely meet the legal requirement to put it in for its annual MOT to check road-worthiness.

Pulling away in first gear is the quickest, easiest one to use when:

- you are the new leader of a team;
- the company is going through change;
- new people join your team;
- the adverse behaviour of a team member needs sorting out.

But you can only go so far in first gear before your engine cries out for you to move to second gear. Driving your car in first gear all the time would not be good at all. Again you could do the car damage and not get very far.

Now engage second gear (Mobilising). Having planned your route and pulled off in first gear, you are now picking up speed and engaging second gear. This is when things change.

- Rather than planning ahead and preparing, at this stage you have to respond, moment by moment, as things occur. You are alert to everything happening on the road as you travel.
- You make your actions very clear, indicating whenever you need to overtake or make a turn. Things can go badly wrong if you fail to show other drivers your intentions clearly.
- Observing the rules of the road and driver etiquette are key to safe travelling.
- This is a time of action, awareness and momentum; a time for being present.

In normal conditions, holding your car in second gear cannot be sustained. As you gain speed, you will need to move up a gear. By listening to your engine and observing the current conditions you know exactly when to do this. Don't worry if it is not clear to you when you make this gear change; we go into it more in Chapter 6.

You're now in third gear (Developing). This is the gear to adopt as you start settling into the journey. Traffic is flowing nicely. You are alert and aware, but are not having to make so many minute adjustments. Usually you don't have to spend too long in this gear before moving smoothly into fourth gear.

If you keep your car in third gear when it's ready to go into fourth, typically your engine will sound as if it's working too hard, you will not go as far and fast as you would like, and it is imperative to change gear for optimum fuel consumption and engine performance.

Many leaders get stuck in third gear and I'm really hoping this analogy will help you to see how vital it is to move things on. At this point you will notice such a difference in your people, as well as possibly becoming aware of a difference to the amount of time you have for strategic planning, business development and marketing.

Into fourth gear (Enabling). When you do change into fourth gear there is a dramatic difference in your engine, and you reach a great place in your journey. You are covering distance now and your engine is in sync. You are keeping a careful eye on things and movements are fluid. You're cruising in fourth gear and covering ground, pressing on to your destination, and your car is very responsive.

At any point during this stage you are ready to take rapid action if the situation ahead changes. Sometimes you might have to drop back to third gear; sometimes more dramatic action is needed, like an emergency stop.

Developing your style as leader is just like this. It needs constant attention. It is not a one-off learning experience.

By listening to your engine, you will know exactly when to move up or down a gear. Just like driving a car, the 4 Step Process needs practice to make the gear changes smooth. We'll look at the skills needed at each stage in the next chapter.

At this point I just want you to feel what the 4 Step Process is like, and how, once you understand it properly, you will become so tuned to the engine that is your people. You will absolutely know when to switch gear and adapt your style to each and every member of your team.

The Liberating Leadership programme offers leaders the chance to have an MOT – a review of their skills and thinking, and space to fine-tune their approach. When your car has an MOT, usually the engine is sound and you breathe a sigh of relief, but you also know that a new tyre, headlamp or wiper blade can make all the difference to your driving experience and keep your car in tip-top condition. So it is with leaders. You are probably intuitively doing a lot that is good.

Right now you might be able to assess:
- What gear are you in?
- What gear *should* you be in?
- What action could you take that would make a massive difference?

A 'Rum' Case Study

I had the pleasure of going to St Lucia to work with the four directors and twenty-two senior managers of St Lucia Distillers Ltd, an award-winning rum distillery in the scenic Roseau Valley.

The culture of the company was one where there was a dependence on senior management to make all the decisions. There was a general focus on the weaknesses and not the positive attributes of the company. We recognised that management needed to feel empowered and to take responsibility for their own areas and the growth of the company and themselves. We also recognised that we needed to build motivation and team spirit.

MARGARET MONPLAISIR, HR DIRECTOR ST LUCIA DISTILLERS (AT THE TIME)

The training involved taking the directors and managers through the programme, starting with Insights Discovery®, then Liberating Leadership. This was supported with training for their staff using another of our powerful products: *Pioneering Professional: self-directing skills for life.*

It took two weeks of being on site, running training or one-to-one coaching every day with the two groups to get them through in the quickest time. I had a fabulous time with them all and really felt there had been some fundamental shifts in behaviour.

On the day I left, I received perfect confirmation of this, which made my heart sing. As I got to the gate to meet my taxi, the gateman came out of his box smiling, and said he wanted to shake my hand and thank me. I asked him why.

He said, 'You've been training the managers here, and they're already treating me differently.'

'In what way?' I asked.

'They're being kinder!'

'Like how?'

He said, 'Like on Friday, going out the gate one of them wound down his window as he drove through and said "Have a nice weekend".'

I said, 'Surely they've said that before?'

He said, 'Yes...but this time he looked at me properly and said it as if he really meant it.'

This is why I love doing what I do.

Another beautiful example comes from one of the Liberating Leadership practitioners who realised she had used the 4 Step Process to help her achieve her own personal goals. The following story is a gift from Nicky Cowling of Good Day Yellow Ltd.

How to lead yourself through the Steps

'Earlier this year, at the Easter Bunny 10k Run in Somerset I recorded a time of 59 minutes and 38 seconds. A remarkable time – absolutely not. A remarkable time for me – absolutely!

At a recent meeting of Liberating Leadership practitioners, we were asked to talk about our successes, and this achievement was very much on top for me. Initially I couldn't see how it had any relevance for the work we do with teams and their leaders. On reflection I realised that the process that I had applied, to turn myself from someone who would avoid running at all costs into someone who intends to be running for a very long time, was exactly the leadership process we advocate.

It started with the Visioning stage at a dinner party and a discussion with friends about getting older. Sound familiar? This led to my vision (it actually sounded much more like a declaration of defiance at the dinner party) to enter my fifties with a positive view of the decade to come and a belief that anything I can do (and wear) in my forties, I'll be able to continue in my fifties.

At the root of the declaration was actually something much deeper: a fear of being left behind by my other half; something I have seen happen to other couples where one stays fit and active and the other struggles with weight and health problems in later life. My vision is for us to be climbing the mountain together (or at least walking up big hills) when we retire.

With hindsight, the leadership behaviour of projecting what you stand for has consistently been one of the most influential. If I hadn't told so many people what I was planning to achieve at this stage, I might well have given up.

Analysing my starting point, another important skill, was more straightforward: I was too much of a couch potato. I had to accept that I needed to become more active.

The Mobilising stage was interesting. This is the stage in the leadership process where you get others on board and ensure that they are clear about their part in your plan. I knew that I needed some clear goals to keep me on track, one of which was to run a 10k in under an hour before my birthday.

Being assertive and direct with myself, doing the positive self talk that got me out the front door after the ice had barely thawed in December was a challenge, as was accepting the clear feedback that my watch provided. I just wasn't running fast enough. I needed to step outside of my comfort zone and train with other people.

The Developing stage is all about motivation, both to start something new and to keep going, and choosing the right style of development activity to match the individual and the challenge they face. For me this involved joined a running club and running with other people.

This has been the most illuminating part of the experience. To start with I failed to breathe properly because I was embarrassed at the thought of other people hearing me gasping for oxygen. Losing my inhibitions and giving myself permission not to sound and look 'normal' in company was a big challenge.

The style of the development has been critical. Too much support and I feel patronised, too little challenge and nothing changes. I've learnt so much about what motivates me and just how easily I allow doubts about my own ability to hold me back.

I ran my first race (since the leapfrog relay in my last year at primary school) in January in a time of 60 minutes and 5 seconds. If I hadn't expended so much energy during that race worrying about how I would feel if I came last I might have achieved my goal at that point. As it was I got there at Easter, a good outcome as I got to eat a guilt free chocolate egg as part of the celebration.

The final Enabling stage of the leadership process is about building capability in the best way for each team member and recognising the right point to let go of control, whilst at the same time maintaining support and encouragement. In the past I have been guilty of letting newly established good habits lapse once the 'big goal' has been achieved. Anyone who has yo-yo dieted will recognise this behaviour.

In order to complete the leadership process I needed to revisit the original vision and work out how to maintain my new fitness levels and set new goals to keep me motivated.

As part of a running club it's easy to get caught up in the view that faster and further is better, but this approach to building capability was not relevant for me. At the Ivybridge 10k I knocked another 32 seconds off my time, not because I was aiming to go faster, but with the aim of getting a T-shirt and trying to enjoy myself.

My new goal is to run 10km (entering at least one more race!)

fifty times before I'm fifty-one. It is about building capability through consistency. And I've told you, so now I'll have to do it.

Recognising the personal impact that the Liberating Leadership process has had for me, both now and in terms of how I see the future, has reinforced my confidence in the approach, and also reminded me that we can expect a few blisters on the way to success.

As a leader, it's constantly important to do your best to put yourself in the shoes of your followers. Perhaps the most effective way to do this is to apply this leadership process to your own behaviour.'

NICKY COWLING, DIRECTOR, GOOD DAY YELLOW
WWW.GOODDAYYELLOW.CO.UK

THE SKILLS

The 15 skills that matter
Chunk them, step by step – all will be revealed
Putting everything together so far
The Competency Wheel

3 | **THE STEPS**

4 | **THE SKILLS**

5 | **THE SECRETS**

THE SKILLS

The 15 skills that matter

Fifteen might sound like a lot to you, but don't let this faze you – you definitely don't need to use them all at once. Also, they don't all need to be perfect all the time. Understanding what they are and when you need them, and keeping them fit for purpose and maintained so they are ready when you need them, with perhaps a little brush up, is important.

The 15 Skills are described clearly in our *Liberating Leadership* book, and my aim here in *Insights into Liberating Leadership* is to give you a flavour of their importance, some stories around them to bring them to life, and ideas on how you might use them.

The beauty of these particular skills is that they are the generic skills of high performing leaders. My clients love them because they fit with most in-house competency systems. They fit because they are needed by all leaders, in a company of any size, in any market sector.

I have introduced them to heads and deputies in education, to the leaders of charities, to an all-inclusive resort and a renowned rum distillery, a range of small private companies in the UK, as well as to leaders in the NHS. When I do executive coaching I always introduce my clients to the programme if they are responsible for leading a team, and I'll give you a fabulous example of how this works.

Recently I coached a young salesman, Tom, who had joined a global organisation at quite a high level because of his ability to sell and his specialised technical knowledge. The reason he joined was because the smaller almost family-run business he had grown up in since leaving university had been bought by the bigger organisation. Tom hadn't had any formal leadership training. He had been busy learning his craft and helping to run the small office. Now in this mammoth organisation most of the managers had received extensive leadership training over the years. Tom needed to be graded on their well-established Leadership Talent Matrix after the initial 'honeymoon' period was over, and the need for rapid coaching was compelling.

But there were two problems:

1   His director, Chris, who had mentored him for so long, had strong Fiery Red energy. He was authoritative, action-oriented and voluble in meetings, and was going to retire in two years, as agreed in the buy-out. Tom was predominantly Earth Green, quieter and more restrained, and wasn't visible in meetings, especially when Chris was there too. He desperately needed to be recognised by the global leaders and potentially fill Chris's shoes.

2   Tom didn't even want to look at the Leadership Talent Matrix. It looked too daunting for words – he preferred to be out on location, selling to customers.

So the goal in coaching Tom was to make him stand out, be visible in his own right whether or not Chris was in the room, and enable Chris to grade him on the Leadership Talent Matrix. The five categories on the matrix ranged from 'leadership improvement needed' to 'highest leadership talent', and currently Tom was 'un-gradable' – not even close to being in the first category.

Over eight months, in a series of 3-hour sessions I took Tom through Insights Discovery® and the Liberating Leadership programme. He immediately understood how his personality was impacting on things and really started to enjoy learning the skills of high performing leaders, even though it was a steep learning curve for him.

Part way through, I received this feedback from Chris in an email to me:

'I have absolutely noticed a difference in Tom... He made an outstanding job of presenting his bit in our mid-year review a couple of weeks ago. In the dry run the day before presenting to the big bosses, we all looked at Tom as if to ask, where the hell did that come from? He just smashed it... I'm not sure what you are doing to him... he really is stepping up to the mark, almost a new Tom. It was not apparent in his manner previously, so I can only think that you have managed to have an effect straight off the bat...quite amazing.

The coaching programme is more beneficial than I had expected by far, and you caught him at exactly the right moment. He's almost instantly having to put what he's learned into practice... the way he is conducting himself as a manager is a stunning improvement at this stage... he's exceeding my expectations.'

And by the end of the coaching, Tom was graded in the top box for leadership talent and put forward for fast-tracking through the company's global management programme, as well as being asked to participate in corporate strategic planning.

Chris said: 'Tom is really taking charge of his responsibilities now and being firm with people in both spoken and written word. He's doing a great job. He got called into one of the European offices to help sort out a dysfunctional team. When I asked the local manager if Tom's input was helping, he gave him a blinding review, saying Tom was helping to restore order and that his motivational and structured approach was really appreciated.'

Result!

You might be wondering what Tom is feeling now... Well, he's chuffed to bits that he's getting the recognition.

Tom was so incredibly successful in just eight months because he understood himself and paid attention to the page on *Suggestions for Development* in his Insights Discovery® profile. Then he got into the mindset, worked the process and rigorously applied the fifteen generic skills of high performing leaders.

Chunk them step by step – all is now revealed

Let's have a look at these 15 Skills. Firstly, they are neatly chunked and flow through the 4 Step Process. Just like with driving a car, your focus needs to change according to the gear you are in. We will therefore chunk them, step by step, before your eyes.

These are the skills Tom took on board.

Step 1 – Visioning. Interestingly, this first part of the process is one which leaders are generally not very good at. Maybe they feel they need to get going with some action and don't take time to think about it clearly enough. Maybe it's not something they have ever thought about before. You start by:

1 **Demonstrating a clear, personal style.** You are visible to people, in the office, walking round, or by some virtual means. You are setting the ground rules and boundaries, giving people a sense of safety. Because you are there, they know you are paying attention and are alert to things.

2 Taking time to **observe what is currently going on** – how people are feeling and behaving. You are aware of the climate and can sense any undercurrents or unrest.

3 Having carefully observed what's going on, you **analyse the situation accurately**. People know you can see and understand; you get them, and they can see this. You know the action you are going to take, which comes through your vision.

4 **Capturing your vision and sharing it with the team**, so everyone knows where they are heading. It's strong, vibrant and unequivocal. Hopefully you will have thought about this already, as it is also one of the elements which underpins The Crux, which we talked about in Chapter 2.

Having set your stall out through your vision it then needs implementing, so you move up a gear.

Step 2 – Mobilising. This is really like mobilising your troops (as I imagine it, although I can't specifically claim to have led an army). 'This is where we're heading, and this is how we're going to get there'.

5   Now the need is to be very clear about the way you want things done. **You are so explicit**, people can't fail to understand, and if they do fail to understand, you explain in ever clearer terms until they get it.

6   Having been very explicit about what you want done and how, it makes it easy for you to **give feedback** on each person's behaviour so that they know how they're doing.

7   You are great at **maintaining momentum** – keeping things going, picking up speed so that you can shortly change gear again. It wouldn't do to get stuck in this step for too long; it would be exhausting for you, and you would never be free to do the more strategic stuff.

8   To operate well at this stage, you need a level of **authority and assertiveness** to push your remarkable engine of people on, otherwise they will realise you are not really serious and soon slip back. They like to push the boundaries and see if there are any weak points. You need to be in good shape, ready to deal with these instances.

9   You are **good at understanding why people behave as they do**, because you use the trusted Performance Navigator, the special diagnostic flowchart which comes with the Liberating Leadership programme. This chart guides you, ensures you leave nothing to chance, and enables you to bring about the changes needed through improving the skills and attitudes of your people. They either have to move up or out, and quickly.

With the team focused on your vision, doing things the way you want and how you want with a high level of skill and will, you definitely need to change gear again. Holding them back can do damage. You'll be accused of micro-managing. Indeed, some people would get disenchanted and seem to go backwards or become completely dependent on you; others would leave because you keep getting in the way. You don't want any of this to happen, so it's time to move up a gear again.

Step 3 – Developing.

10 You can afford to **flex your style**. You understand the gear changes needed for optimum speed and performance, you are able to deal effectively with varying levels of skill and commitment to achieving the overall vision. You reward the team members who work hard and progress well, you encourage those who are trying hard but are still finding things difficult.

11 **Knowing how to motivate** each and every person in the team is now key, and you absolutely know what rewards will motivate them. For instance, one might appreciate time off for working hard to complete a job. Another who lives for work would find that totally demotivating and would prefer having increased responsibility to make them feel good and keep them engaged.

12 At this stage in the process you are **generating continuous improvement** through accepting responsibility for mistakes and dealing with them as learning opportunities for people. You know how much to become personally involved.

A good example for you here is when I was making a sponge cake with my nine-year-old son. We had made cakes often before, but not for a little while, and this time we were in a rush. I cracked the first egg into the mixture. He cracked the second, but rammed it so hard on the side of the bowl it spilled everywhere. He looked at it in dismay.

I quickly scooped up the mess, popped it in the bowl, and said, 'Go on, crack the third egg.'

He said, 'You've got to be joking!'

Even though I was desperate to grab the third egg and do it because time was of the essence, I encouraged him to carry on, saying, 'Go on, you'll be fine with this one', and, of course, he was.

If I had cracked the third egg, my son would never have learnt to make a cake by himself. This is what the Developing stage is all about: you are there to develop and support, not take over, even though you can and often want to. It's a lovely stage to be in. You have a great relationship with your team; the relationship is easy and more of a two-way thing than in the first two stages, and far too many leaders get stuck here instead of pushing for excellence.

Going back to the car analogy, what would happen if you kept driving with your car in third gear? Yes, your engine would be working too hard. It would be willing you to change into fourth gear for the smoothest ride and to relieve pressure on the engine.

Changing gear again now is the only way to achieve optimum performance.

The task of leadership is not to put greatness into people, but to elicit it, for the greatness is there already.

JOHN BUCHAN

Step 4 — Enabling. This final step is absolutely brilliant for team members, which leaders intuitively know, but it is arguably the hardest one of all for the leader. This is another reason they like to settle at Step 3, but here at Step 4 these are the skills:

13 You have now **totally empowered** your team members to do their job by building their skill, will and confidence, and you now need to let them get on with it and stop meddling.

Now my son doesn't need me to make a cake with him. He understands recipes, he knows what he's doing, he can make his own meals without my interference, he can make judgements about what will work and what won't. I catch my breath and think, Oh, what do I do now? Maybe now is the time to write a book!

14 Even though a team member might not think they are ready, you expertly judge when to push them on gently. You **delegate complete authority** for a task so the team member can own it; you retain overall responsibility, and only intervene when absolutely necessary.

15 Of course, you are always there to provide **support and encouragement**, reinforcing and developing each team member's capability. Some members of the team may leave at this point because they are good to go, ready to take on their own team. They want to give others the same fabulous chance that they've had, and they want to do it like you.

This means you may need to recruit someone new, and you know now that starting in Step 1 will get you both off to the quickest and best start.

As with driving a car, it is not always a smooth ride as you move through the gears from first to fourth. There may be an obstacle in the road, you may have to change down to second or third gear to help you get round it, or you may even have to stop and start again in first gear. As a driver, you are constantly responding to what it is happening around you — sometimes you even need to reverse.

It is the same for leaders. Rather than limiting yourself and your team by becoming stuck in your own preferred way of doing things, you appreciate there are more gears to engage to drive towards continuous improvement and, at same time, make your role more fulfilling. You will realise the pure joy of leading a team of people.

When the best leader's work is done the people say: "We did it ourselves."

LAO TZU

Putting things together so far

Let's pause for a moment. There's been a lot of information to take in, so we'll have a little review of the story so far.

Holding up the Mirror

I am sure you can now see how your personality style colours your leadership style, and how all four Insights colour energies flow through the 4 Step Process. The greatest leaders tap into all four colours, but the truth is that most of us get comfortable with one or two.

The Crux

The whole system will fall over if you fail to work on the elements which make up The Crux. Luckily the first two elements which underpin The Crux – setting your vision clearly and establishing the ground rules – are two of the skills needed at the start of the process. Then you work on achieving the sweet spot for leaders, which is getting High Challenge and High Support in powerful and equal balance. You have high expectations of what people can achieve and constantly reinforce the behaviour you want to see. You act at all times with a positive belief in people; you only need to comment on behaviour rather than put the whole person down in your mind. And you are genuinely able to give people frank, honest feedback.

I don't know if you have ever been on the receiving end of feedback which has not been done with Positive Regard. I have, and it's really not nice.

When it happened to me, I wondered why the person was bothering to give me feedback, especially when the feedback was ostensibly good. It was unsettling and annoying; I just wanted to keep out the way so I didn't have to hear it. This wasn't great in a small company where we needed to be working well together.

The 4 Step Process

In the 4 Step Process, **Step 1 is Visioning** – where you set the ground rules, the contract, sense the mood. **Step 2 is Mobilising** – where you are explicit about what you want done and how to do it, maintain momentum by giving constant feedback, especially where you spot people doing something right, and nip any under performance in the bud using the flowchart.

These are the transactional stages which take a lot of your time. This is what management is all about. Then you switch gear, because now come the transformational leadership steps, where it becomes easier for you as you encourage your staff to shine.

In **Step 3 – Developing** – you can flex your style and reward people appropriately, because you know exactly how they tick. You can also give them increasing levels of responsibility, before moving into **Step 4 – Enabling** – where you enable and empower others, handing over complete ownership of a task. They become the master of it, and you drive continuous improvement through support and encouragement, taking your vision higher and further forward, striving for the next level.

Managers light a fire beneath…leaders light a fire within.

EVELYN KAY, ENTHEOS

The Powerful Set of Skills

There are fifteen generic leadership skills which you need:

1   Be clear about your style. Be the leader you want to be, and make it visible.

2   Observe the current climate in your team.

3   Analyse the situation correctly.

4   Set your vision and share it.

5   Be explicit about what you want done and how you want it done.

6   Catch people doing something right, give feedback every day to improve performance

7   Keep on top of things; maintain momentum so that nothing slips.

8   Maintain a level of detached assertiveness to push boundaries, challenge and support.

9   Understand why people behave the way they do and take appropriate action.

10 Flex your style according to how each team member is performing.

11 Understand what motivates each person in your team and reward appropriately.

12 Generate continuous improvement, know how much to become personally involved.

13 Empower people to get on.

14 Delegate complete task ownership and authority, intervene only when necessary.

15 Provide continuous support, encouragement and challenge.

The Competency Wheel

The way everything fits together is in a wheel, and this time we'll use the analogy of a bicycle wheel.

Imagine:

- at the centre of the wheel you have The Crux – your vision, ground rules, mindset;
- the rim is the 4 Step Process – your overall sense of direction within which everything is held;
- the spokes are the 15 Skills or competencies of high performing leaders

Like this:

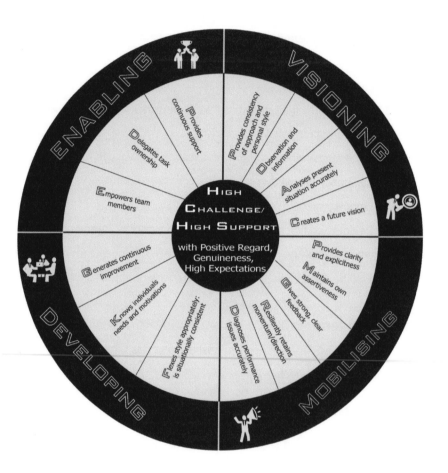

The solid hub in the middle of the wheel is vital. You *could* understand the 4 Step Process, and have a pretty good grasp of the 15 Skills, but if you don't have the right underlying mindset, if you are acting without *Positive Regard* and *Genuineness*, there is nothing to anchor the spokes and at some point the wheel will collapse. The leader is seen as a fraud. They leave, or things go badly wrong and the people leave.

If you have developed the central mindset, have an overall sense of the process, then you can have the odd rusty skill or 'spoke' and the wheel will hold good. People understand what you are doing and why, and they appreciate you are human and can make mistakes.

THE SECRETS

Learn the secrets:
Secret No 1: Explicitness
Secret No 2: Remote and approachable
Secret No 3: Catch someone doing something right
Secret No 4: Performance Navigator
Learning from the best

4 | THE SKILLS

5 | THE SECRETS

6 | THE GEAR CHANGE

THE SECRETS

Learn the Secrets

We call them 'secrets' because they're rarely taught. There are four secrets, and they all appear at Step 2, the Mobilising phase of the process. If you currently lead people, take these to heart and try them out immediately, at work and at home. They will bring the quickest wins.

Secret 1: Explicitness

Time and again when I am training trainers to deliver the Liberating Leadership programme, they say that explicitness was the single most important mind shift or skill. They have used it to great effect to get better results with their children, their own team, and one even said it worked for her cleaner. Up until then, the cleaner had just been pushing a hoover around and not doing the other jobs that were needed, annoying my colleague, Jane, to death in the process. Being explicit was the key needed for her to detach emotionally and explain very clearly what was needed.

You might wonder why the cleaner had not been told before, but what Jane was doing was another trap leaders often fall into. She had believed the cleaner was deliberately avoiding doing things like dusting the skirting boards and cleaning the windows. Why couldn't the cleaner see they needed doing, and why should she have to be told? Surely any self-respecting cleaner would just get on with it.

There are a couple of other traps around lack of explicitness – see which one applies to you:

- Some leaders assume a level of competence in a new employee based on their qualifications, what they put on their CV or said in the interview. The leader thinks it may be patronising to tell the person what's needed, because if they have done a certain kind of job before they should be able to get on with it now, or work out how to do things by having a go. They clearly have the skill; that's why you employed them.

- Others are too vague and get seriously disappointed when people don't live up to expectations. For example:

A trainer called Kim, who attended one of my programmes, was getting hot under the collar with her admin assistant. She had asked the assistant several times to go out into the reception area when customers came in and use her initiative. The assistant would use her initiative by tidying up the magazines, taking away empty cups, and leaving the clients to their own thoughts.

What Kim meant by 'using her initiative' was for the assistant to go out and talk to the clients, tell them they wouldn't be kept waiting long, ask how their day was going so far, etc. The assistant does this now.

Jim, a director, wanted his staff to be passionate – and was disgruntled because they weren't. I asked him what he meant by 'being passionate'. As one of his employees, how would I be showing him I was passionate? What would I be doing to indicate this?

I gave him the example of an employee who is clearly showing passion by consistently arriving early, often working late to finish a piece of work, not taking long lunch hours and rarely being off sick.

Jim said, 'No, that's not passion! I need them to be smiling when they're talking to clients. I want them to go the extra mile and buy flowers to put in the new houses to greet people as they walk in. I want them to come up with new ideas about how we can do things.'

When I asked if he had ever shared this with his employees before, he said no. He had expected them to get this without him having to say, assuming it was common sense.

Just to change tack slightly, if you are a parent, have you ever said to your child, 'Tidy your room', only to go back an hour or so later and see that nothing much has been done? You are disappointed with what you see, but the child protests that they have tidied it. Well, in their model of the world maybe they have, but certainly not yours.

So, if you want the room tidied the way you want it, you have to be explicit. 'By *tidy* I mean put your toys away in the toy box, put your clothes away in your drawers, make your bed, clear your tops leaving only your clock, your ornaments and essential items. There should be nothing on your floor apart from your feet, your furniture and your football. I will be back in one hour – does that give you enough time?'

How explicit are you in the instructions you give to your people?

What could you do to improve this further?

Explicitness is needed especially

- in the early stages of the leadership process
- when you introduce a new way of working
- in times of great change

In these situations, the more explicit you can be about what is going on and why, the more relaxed your people will be, enabling them to continue with their work instead of worrying.

I've got a great acronym, which should very much be part of any leader's skill set:

L	=	Lead
E	=	Explicitly
A	=	And
D	=	Deliver
E	=	Excellent
R	=	Results

Secret 2: Remote and Approachable

By 'remote' I mean being slightly detached rather than being too distant.

The only way you can give strong, clear feedback that will be interpreted correctly by the individual is to be Remote and Approachable. This means not always going out for lunch with them or for a drink after work, you just do this sometimes. Your people need time to gel together without you, and if you as leader are feeling left out, you need to find peers to connect with.

I'm not suggesting here that you create a hierarchical command and control type of culture – far from it. This is a relationship based on High

Challenge and High Support, Positive Regard and Genuineness. Your role is to develop your people, and you are likely to build more dependency rather than independency if everything is too cosy. And remember, we are talking about the early stages of the leadership process, Steps 1 and 2. This is not needed in the later stages when there is more of a partnership relationship going on.

So, in these early stages, and especially when a leader is new to a team or has been promoted from within, what we find is that some leaders can be too friendly with their people. If the boundaries are fudged in this way, it makes corrective feedback more difficult. Leaders either shy away from doing it or dress it up with niceties: 'Sorry to bring this up, but if you wouldn't mind not doing that again, that would be great.'

What also happens is that this can develop into a shared blame culture, where you skirt around the issue to make things better. Maybe you moan about clients or suppliers who are making things difficult for you all. If it wasn't for the way they were behaving, you are sure the team member would be able to do things properly. You are deflecting blame elsewhere instead of tackling the issue head on. This can be experienced as being too supporting; the atmosphere is nice, everyone is getting along, but you are not achieving the results you imagined. Also, you won't have the best relationship with those you are blaming.

At the other extreme, leaders can be too distant or superior with people. Their feedback can come across as a directive: 'If I see you doing that again, you'll be sorry.'

I've come across several companies where this is happening all the time. The leader is more autocratic, blowing up at the least little thing in their drive for perfection. When anything happens, an edict is sent by email: 'From now on, all expenses must be submitted by 28th of each month, otherwise you will not be reimbursed.'

Team members become worn down, their good work isn't recognised. The leader's interest is clearly not in them as a person, only in systems, procedures and bottom line performance. It is definitely an overly challenging culture, and it leads to stress for all.

In the Remote and Approachable space, you are using Positive Regard and Genuineness. You will notice that Genuineness is missing from the first example, and Positive Regard from the second. So the type of feedback you might give is: 'Rather than doing what you did, it would be even better if you did this. This will help us to achieve our goals.'

In this state, people feel safe and appropriately challenged. They know what to do to improve and why. They know they can come and talk to you if they get stuck or need clarification because you are approachable without being a 'soft touch'.

Secret 3: Catch someone doing something right

If ever leaders don't know where to start because so much seems to be going wrong, I tell them to notice and comment on everything that is going right for the next two weeks. Forget what's going wrong for the moment; we can work out a plan for dealing with that by using the next secret tool.

To **catch people doing something right** is a skill you might have to cultivate, because the norm is to take what people do well for granted. That's what you pay them to come in and do, so you only comment when things go wrong.

What sometimes happens when you start catching people doing

something right is that it can become glib and patronising: 'Well done', 'Well done', 'Hey, well done'. It's a little bit like using the Insights Discovery® colour energies superficially – 'I can't do that because I'm a Yellow'. Your praise could sound insincere if you say 'Thank you' or 'Well done' too much.

Again, we are still in the early stages of the 4 Step Process. Your use of this 'catch people doing something right' skill is to try and turn round poor behaviour or improve already good behaviour.

For instance, when helping my son Sam to turn round his unruly behaviour, we agreed all sorts of rules which included sorting out his personal as well as school life. One of the rules was to have his washing in the washing basket (placed conveniently outside his bedroom door) by 7pm every Friday evening.

The first thing to be aware of when you set a rule or a goal to correct performance is that you have to be there to notice it happening. Be prepared, it takes a lot of your time, but it is the essential underpinning work for success.

So in this situation where Sam needs to put his washing in the basket by 7pm on a Friday, I have to be there every Friday evening to notice whether this is happening or not. I need to take action to ensure it a) gets going or b) keeps happening.

As the saying goes, 'What gets measured, gets done'.

If I was not around to notice each Friday, then Sam's washing would stay scattered around his bedroom. In Sam's mind this doesn't matter, because I'm clearly not serious about it, and he's not being punished.

The second point is, it really pays to question the talk going on in your head, and be careful with what you say. On the first Friday evening, shortly after 7pm when I checked the contents of the washing basket, I wanted to shout 'Halleluiah, I have only waited for *fifteen* years for this to happen!' in a condescending way. But I checked myself, popped my head round his door, and said, 'Brilliant, well done, Sam. If you do that again next Friday we'll be on a roll!' He held up his hand so we could do a high five and we were on our way.

If this resonates with you then I challenge you now to give it a go and see what difference it makes. In the first instance, just notice what happens and record it. I would love it if you would then share your results with me.

Secret 4: Performance Navigator

The Performance Navigator is a flowchart in the *Liberating Leadership* book. It is so amazing, many clients look at it and ask if they can buy just that page, blow it up and put it on their wall.

I have now made it available via my website www.alistewartandco.com. Sign up for it on the Liberating Leadership page, and it will be sent to you along with guidance notes on how to use it. And it is available as an A3 poster, so you can put it on the wall.

The Performance Navigator is structured and simple. That does not mean it doesn't take time, hard work and input from you, because it certainly does. But it enables you to relax, knowing you are working within a structure or process.

There is a definite starting point and end point. You decide how quickly you can or need to get through it, you define the end date. You need resilience to see it through to conclusion, and when you do it is incredibly rewarding – rewarding for you and for the person involved in the review.

The end point can only be one of two things:

1   The person is now performing well, you are rewarding the improved behaviour through feedback and maintaining momentum, and everyone is happy for the time being.

2   The person must go because they don't have either the necessary level of skill for the role or the right attitude. When I say 'go' I mean you move them to a more suitable position if you have one, or their position is terminated and you do what you can to help them on their way.

Even if at the final count you do need to remove a team member, our experience is that by the time you have gone through the Performance Navigator with them and things are still not working, they will be relieved and leave gracefully on good terms. You have both tried hard to make it work.

The skill of working through the Performance Navigator will stand you in good stead. The process stands up to scrutiny, and clients love it because it flows into their performance management system, as well as disciplinary and grievance procedures, and stands up to tribunal. HR departments love it because they can see leaders are operating to a proper system and not leaving things to chance. They know where they are every step of the way, can explain why they're there and what action they're taking.

It takes the heat and emotion out of situations where the performance of a team member may be less than desirable. Instead of their misdemeanours causing you stress, this Performance Navigator helps to bring order and calm things down. It also brings a sense of urgency and closure, rather than allowing poor situations to drag on and your attitude towards the person deteriorating.

You can request the chart today by popping onto www.alistewartandco.com.

Learn from the best

The best way of learning is through *modelling*. Modelling is to copy the behaviour of others who are expert at doing the thing you want to be able to do. Observe what they look like, their facial expressions and movements, what they say, how that act, what they do. Adopt those behaviours, make them work for you, practise them every day, and soon they will feel natural. All athletes watch footage of races over and over again. They watch themselves, they watch others, and they improve their stride, their stroke, their jump through hours of observation and practice.

As Ghandi said, 'Be the change you want to see in the world.'

I was talking with my younger son, Rory. We were reviewing his end of term report before he went into the final GCSE year. He is taking a GCSE in PE, which involves physical sports and theory and was predicted a grade B in both. The teacher had written that Rory could be brilliant if he didn't keep allowing himself to get distracted.

I asked Rory what was distracting him in PE, which I know he loves. He said it was the other boys talking, and the banter that goes on in class, and especially out on the training field. He also said, 'I really want to do well and wish they would all shut up and listen.'

Ah, *they!* 'Be the change you want to see... 'was entirely appropriate here and I said this to Rory. He got it immediately.

'Oh! I've got to shut up and listen, and if I do it will encourage them to do the same?' Yes, it was a lovely light bulb moment. He'll get an A grade now.

Another way to learn is to watch movies. It can't get any easier than that!

I often set this as homework during the Liberating Leadership programme, being the hard task-master that I am. You can draw so much energy, learning and courage for building high performing people and teams from films. There are two I normally rave about: if you have seen them before, you could watch again and this time you'll have your new *Insights into Liberating Leadership* hat on. You will now be looking for:

The Crux – ground rules and vision, High Challenge/High Support, trust, respect, high expectations and reinforcement of wanted behaviours.

The 4 Step Process:
- **Step 1 – Visioning:** watch for the visibility of the leader in the story, their level of observation, correct analysis, clear shared vision.
- **Step 2 – Mobilising:** being explicit about what needs to done, the leader being assertive, giving constant feedback, maintaining momentum and picking up on poor performance by nipping it in the bud.
- **Step 3 – Developing:** the leader flexes their style when the learner(s) taps into their own internal motivation to do the task.

The leader understands how to motivate the learner to keep going and generates continuous improvement by becoming involved only when necessary.

- **Step 4 – Enabling:** the leader completely empowers the learner, delegates total task ownership and provides constant support and encouragement, leading the learner to the next level.

The first film is *Coach Carter*. Samuel L Jackson, in his portrayal of real life coach, Ken Carter, demonstrates a perfect walk through of the Liberating Leadership process, including getting The Crux, which you'll remember is the critical underlying mindset, absolutely right. The way he introduces respect (by expecting his people to call each other Sir) and sets his expectations high is brilliant. He says something like: 'As of now we are a team of winners. If we act like winners, we'll be winners, we are winners. The losing stops now.'

Coach Carter is the film to watch if you want to see an extroverted leader sort out a very unruly team. Coach Carter's visibility of personal style is so strong, the way he sets the ground rules and vision for the team is exemplary. The way he *Mobilises,* or teaches the team the skills of basketball, is funny. The way he pushes the team into the *Developing* stage is masterful. The way the team responds is stunning. The way Coach Carter stands by his values is powerful – but made easy because his vision was so clear. The *Enabled* stage comes when he sees the young men graduate – his work is done.

The other similarly powerful film is the original *Karate Kid* with Pat Morita as Mr Miyagi and Ralph Macchio as Daniel. This is the perfect example of the process with one introverted leader to one learner. Mr Miyagi's visibility of personal style, his observation, his analysis, is equally strong in its quietness. And then the way he sets the vision and the ground rules is calm and clear: the goal is to teach Daniel enough karate for him to be able to fight in the tournament. Mr Miyagi says, 'I promise to teach you Karate; you do what I say without question.' It doesn't get any clearer than that, and Daniel agrees.

In the Mobilising phase Mr Miyagi starts by teaching Daniel how to build the muscle and stamina for Karate in a very explicit but unusual way. He first tells Daniel to wax the cars and demonstrates clearly how to 'wax on' and 'wax off'. Every time Mr Miyagi goes past Daniel he gives him feedback. 'Very good, Daniel San,' he says, if Daniel is waxing on and off correctly. But if Daniel is just rubbing the cloth over the cars any old how, Mr Miyagi stops him and shows him, 'Wax on, wax off, like this'.

He follows a similar process for teaching Daniel how to paint the fence, sand the decking and paint the house, constantly maintaining momentum. When Daniel angrily throws down his tools ready to leave, believing he is being used as a slave and not learning Karate at all, with appropriate assertiveness Mr Miyagi calls him back. Then when Daniel is 'in' on training and understands what they are doing, Mr Miyagi takes him out to learn balance in the waves on the beach and on the bow of a little rowing boat.

There comes a beautiful point in the film where you see Daniel's internal motivation kick in. Daniel himself pushes Mr Miyagi to the Enabled stage when he realises he has to win the tournament. That wasn't part of the original vision – which was just to be good enough to compete.

Both films are incredibly powerful with fabulous endings. All you then have to do is model the behaviour of Coach Carter or Mr Miyagi, their sense of personal power, clarity of vision and perfect walk through the leadership process.

On the off chance that neither of these float your boat, then perhaps you would prefer to watch Mary Poppins through the lens of Insights into Liberating Leadership and the eight point plan. And if you want to brush up on one of the fifteen powerful skills, then *Kung Fu Panda* is brilliant for understanding how to tap into another's *motivation*!

OK, enough about movies. Let's move on.

6

THE GEAR CHANGE

Know when to change gear
Listen to your engine
My story
Choosing the right step – engaging the right gear
Polo, a magnificent horse from Poland

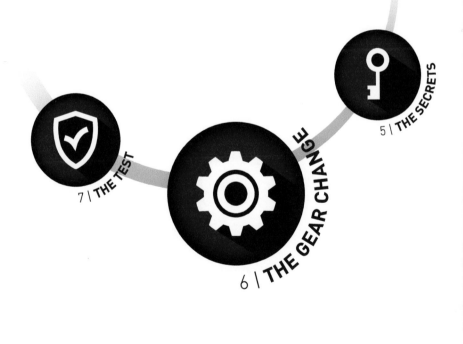

7 | THE TEST

6 | THE GEAR CHANGE

5 | THE SECRETS

THE GEAR CHANGE

Know when to change gear

In Chapter 3 we talked about driving a four gear car and listening to your engine to know when to change gear.

This can seem really easy when driving a car, less so when developing your people. Sometimes you have to change before you are ready so that your people can develop. If you never move on, they can't either.

Before you are leader, success is all about growing yourself; when you become a leader, success is all about growing others.

JACK WELCH

The only problem is you probably became a leader before you even thought about yourself. So learning on the job is required. Those leaders who engage in interpersonal and leadership training, those who have executive coaching and go off on courses and retreats, typically are the more successful, charismatic leaders whom everyone wants to work with. By 'charismatic' I mean more magnetic, charming and captivating.

This is why this eight point plan starts with you holding up the mirror to have a good look at yourself through the lens of the powerful Insights Discovery® model. Then go through an MOT of your leadership skills in a very structured way, going through the elements which make up *The Crux* to develop or even change your mindset.

Polish up *The Skills,* paying attention to ones in need of improvement, as well as *The Secrets,* which are the skills you must have keenly in your grasp.

You will undoubtedly have learnt some skills as you've gone along; some you will have innately. This is now about fine-tuning them to get an even better result.

Most leaders have not tapped into the value of using the 4 Step Process in a dynamic way, like driving a car and constantly changing gear. Often they hold back from changing gear out of fear of the unknown, being content to stay within their comfort zone, or perhaps because they never give it any conscious thought.

In this chapter I'll give you pointers on when to change gear. If ever you change gear too soon, you can always slip back a gear and try again when the climate is better.

Listen to your engine

To listen to your engine – assess where your team member or team is right now – here are some Yes/No questions to guide you:

1 Have I set my vision and do I share it often?

2 Have I set the ground rules?

3 Do team members have the skill and will to do the job?

4 Have I been explicit about the way I want things done?

5 Do my team members have the skill, but they keep checking in with me?

6 Do my team members have the right attitude to work, but lack confidence?

7 Are my team members totally competent, able and performing well?

8 Am I feeling really comfortable with the way things are running right now?

Response Guide:

	Yes	No
1	Great – you should be out of Step 1 and in a different gear	**You are in Step 1 – Visioning** Stop and define your vision and share with all
2	Great – you should be out of Step 1 and in a different gear	**You are in Step 1 – Visioning** Stop and set the ground rules and share with all
3	Great – you should be out of Step 2 and in a different gear	**You are in Step 2 – Mobilising** Get hold of the Performance Navigator flowchart to help you diagnose whether they are lacking the skill or knowledge to do the job, or have the wrong attitude. Take the remedial action shown on the chart, be explicit, give strong, clear feedback, assertively maintain momentum
4	Great – you should be out of Step 2 and at least in Step 3	**You are in Step 2 – Mobilising** Be explicit about what you want done and when, give strong clear feedback, both positive to encourage and negative to correct performance, assertively maintain momentum
5	**You are in Step 3 – Developing** Tap into the person's motivation to encourage and support them, build their confidence and drive continuous improvement – learning is a way of life	You should not be in Step 3. Either they are good to go (Step 4) or you are working on developing their skill or will (Step 2)
6	**You are in Step 3 – Developing** Tap into the person's motivation to encourage and support them, build their confidence and drive continuous improvement – learning is a way of life	You should not be in Step 3. Either they are good to go (Step 4) or you are working on developing their skill or will (Step 2)
7	**You are in Step 4 – Enabling** Congratulations, you have an able team. Give them complete task ownership, delegate even more and provide continuous support	Go to Step 2 – get the Performance Navigator flowchart to work out what is needed right now to drive high performance
8	**You are in Step 4 – Enabling** Congratulations, you have an able team. Decide how you are going lift performance further – yours or theirs!	Go to Step 2 – get the Performance Navigator flowchart to work out what is needed right now to drive high performance

Sometimes you have to shift gear, even if it makes you feel uncomfortable. For instance, some leaders are great at articulating a vision, but don't take action or explain clearly enough how to implement the vision.

Others love doing things for other people and are reluctant to share their knowledge, sometimes because they mistakenly think knowledge is power – they like to be the one who knows everything. They have a high level of skill or qualifications, they are an expert. They like people to keep asking them, it makes them feel important. They don't appreciate that the role of leader is to develop the people.

Then there are those who have developed their people to an extent, or have a team of already skilful people, good at doing their jobs. They have a good relationship with them, but perhaps get too bogged down doing the day to day work. They do too much for the team and don't delegate as much as they should. They get involved with things which the team can sort out perfectly well. They can get stressed, because they don't have enough time to do everything.

> *The best executive is the one who has sense enough to pick good men to do what he wants done, and self-restraint to keep from meddling with them while they do it.*
>
> **THEODORE ROOSEVELT**

As a leader, it is normal to feel a bit wobbly about sharing your relationships, your contacts and some of the work that you think no-one else can do quite as well as you. It is normal to believe you haven't got time to explain and hand over a job to someone else and it is far quicker to do it yourself. Unless you stop and hand things over, you will again be guilty of keeping people in a dependent state.

Give a man a fish and you feed him for a day; teach a man how to fish and you feed him for a lifetime.

CHINESE PROVERB

Listening to your engine means trusting and letting go. If you don't do this, you will never know how to grow or the action you need to take... you will never appreciate the power of your 'engine'.

My story

I was a sole trader, doing *everything* myself and loving it. Well, most parts – doing VAT returns and accounts were a bit tedious. I knew I needed other people, but didn't have time to think about what kind of help I needed, then create roles and write meaningful job descriptions. Also I wasn't sure if I could afford to pay anyone else.

Then my friend Lucy said to me, 'Ali, let me do some work for you. I can take some of the load off you.' So I gave a few bits of admin work to Lucy and paid her for a couple of hours a week. That sounds easy enough, but it was actually the hardest part. I had only just begun and I was definitely suffering growing pains. I had no idea if Lucy was going to do a good job, and I had some fabulous relationships with clients and suppliers which I now had to share. I wasn't sure if I was ready for that.

Before I knew it, I needed more of Lucy's time, needed her to do more things. Then I became acutely aware that to keep up with current trends, a driving business needs to get with Social Media. But that didn't excite or delight me, so I went to see my friend Andy – and he said, 'I'll do it for you.'

So now that a few jobs were being done for me, I was able to do more coaching and training and bring more money in. This was great – except for the weight of receipts and accounts-related things round my neck. I found Keith – a great financial controller and really happy doing book-keeping.

Now back to Lucy. I began to realise that what I was asking her to do was way below her capability. As I became busier, there was more mundane processing to do, and although Lucy was working well, she was wasted doing what she was doing and was hungry for more.

At the same time, Derek, my guide and mentor, said to me, 'Could you use Hayley? She just needs a few hours' work here and there while the children are at school.' Yes, I could. She could take some of the regular processing work off Lucy. Just think, I used to do all that processing work – how crazy was that?

At all times, every member of the team understands their own goals and is working within the guiding mission: to build a sustainable business, provide a unique and powerful service to clients, work only with clients we like and who are ready and committed to take action to achieve their goals.

At times during this growth I was ready and knew the action I needed to take; at other times I listened to the team to see what they needed. It remains an ongoing process. They constantly push me to be a better leader.

When things don't go well, I realise I haven't been explicit enough; haven't paid enough attention to the way things are being done or given sufficient feedback. At such times, I take corrective action and get things back on track.

Because my team members all work remotely and are at the Enabled stage for most tasks, it is vital for me to keep in touch, providing support and encouragement so they know they are appreciated and their work is valued. It would be altogether too easy just to let them get on with it and not comment at all.

To be able to *listen to your engine*, it is essential for you take time out to work on your business instead of in it, and to work on yourself to maintain balance. If you keep your head down, working on tasks all the time, it can lead to stress and burn out or a feeling of emptiness. This is true of some of the leaders I coach, often those high in Fiery Red competitive, demanding energy, who have built successful businesses, but who can often leave a trail of dead bodies in their wake. They become so wrapped up in the task of building their business, they either don't appreciate the importance of taking time out for themselves, or they forget. Often this can be to the detriment of their family, for whom they had been building their business in the first place. They wonder what went wrong, then search for greater meaning in their lives.

Choosing the right step – engaging the right gear

You may have noticed that the questions at the beginning of the chapter how the steps are grouped together. Steps 1 and 2 go together, and Steps 3 and 4 go together. With the car analogy, first and second gears are needed to get the car going and react to what is going on; third and fourth gears enable the car to cover more ground and go further quicker.

In leadership, we call the first two steps *Transactional* leadership or management. This is what you do on a day by day basis: setting and sharing the vision and ground rules, being explicit about the way things are done, giving feedback to get more of the behaviour you want, and assertively keeping performance on track. Steps 1 and 2 take a lot of your time; you need to be there, you need to be present. You are pushing your people forward with vision and momentum.

The third and fourth steps are *Transformational* leadership. Here you are creating a world to which people want to belong. They understand what you are doing and why, and really want to be a part of helping you get there. Steps 3 and 4 take less of your time as team members become more competent and skilled and take on the ownership of tasks. You don't need to meddle in the day to day things, even though you can.

As you will appreciate now, neither Transactional nor Transformational leadership can exist without the other. Often leaders are good in one of these areas, or just the middle two and not the first and last steps.

Frequently I see leaders who:
- don't appreciate their impact on others
- fail to identify the root cause of behaviour and end up treating the wrong thing
- confuse people being busy with people being productive
- haven't learnt the mindset or skills needed for managing and leading people
- get stuck in their own preferred way of doing things, according to their personality style

Knowing when the switch between Transactional and Transformational leadership, between Steps 2 and 3, happens is vital. The move from the very hands-on *Mobilising* stage, where you are teaching skills, telling people, being very clear about how you want things done, to the much more hands-off *Developing* stage, is driven by the people. The idea is, you as leader adapt your style when you notice a change in the person.

It can be very obvious to both of you when you see the penny drop, the person shouts, 'Yes, I've got it, I want to do this now', and you feel the energy shift;

Or just to you when you see they now have the skill and can do it, but they are still a bit hesitant, wanting constant reassurance. Or just to them when they totally get it and tell you to stop interfering!

It is great being in Step 3, more relaxed than in Step 2. People know what they are doing and how to do it, and are motivated because they know you understand them. Usually the relationship between you and them is good. It is more a partnership: you still feel needed and they feel valued. This is why it is so easy to get stuck here and not step up to Step 4.

I urge you to take this final, magical step and move smoothly into fourth gear. You might feel a bit lonely – your people can manage perfectly well without you – but step up to embrace your next goal, your next challenge. Get whatever support you need from your peers or your coach. Be there to support the team and become involved only when necessary.

Leadership is lifting a person's vision to higher sights, the raising of a person's performance to a higher standard, the building of a personality beyond its normal limitations.

PETER F DRUCKER

Polo, a magnificent horse from Poland

The following case study was written for my blog. You might want to grab a cup of tea then read this wonderful true story of Polo, and how Sally Foan of People Tree Training, one of the first practitioners in Liberating Leadership, used the Liberating Leadership method to help him.

Sally's story

As a regular user of Liberating Leadership in my coaching and training, I recently realised how I had subconsciously been using one key element of this amazing programme to good effect in a completely new environment. I also realised it was a good analogy or metaphor to use in my coaching for managers dealing with performance issues, particularly in terms of undesirable behaviour in their team.

Here is my team member. His name is Polo and he is a horse from Poland. He is pretty big, 16hh for those of you who understand how we measure the height of a horse. That's around 64 inches high to the level of his back. His head goes higher still! He probably weighs as much as a medium car. He is bigger and stronger than me and does not speak English. Polo had been sold on often because of his bad behaviour, and no-one really wanted him.

Sometimes in business, we inherit team members with poor behaviours, don't we? I think people may have tried to get Polo to change. Thinking about the methods that Derek shares in his Liberating Leadership book to change behaviour, I think penalties (in this case rapping Polo's legs with poles if he failed to jump a jump) had been used rather a lot, causing fear of poles, and pretty much everything else too. I also think rewards had been used (hand feeding carrots) which caused nipping and biting. Sadly Polo had been beaten to get him on trailers or lorries when he didn't want to go on, and it caused a big problem for us, having him rearing and dragging us around the yard to get away from the trailer. The way we have been treated in the past lingers with us all.

I like a challenge and decided to try to change these behaviours. Also, my instructor (who looked at Polo before I bought him) and I both felt Polo had potential. As in the Liberating Leadership programme, I saw him as he might be, not as he was then. If you look at Derek's flowchart on performance and 'Can do/can't do, Will do/won't do', I believe I was subconsciously looking at this when I began to try to enable change: transformational change.

I built trust by behaving in a consistent way. I looked for, commented on and rewarded what I wanted with a scratch, a kind tone and good, regular, reliable care. When I got something I didn't want I used a negative tone without raising my voice, and certainly no physical punishment. I resisted, wherever I could, any attempt from him to push me around. I did this assertively by physically moving Polo back to his start position and I moved back to mine. I tried hard to maintain a mindset of 'I'm ok/you're ok' even when he was sometimes in an 'I'm ok/you're not ok' or 'I'm not ok/you're not ok' mindset. I did not allow or reward poor behaviours (as that would manifest more of them) and I made sure I noticed good behaviour. I rewarded the 'try' with my tone and some reassuring contact. Cutting out the hand feeding and food bribery resulted in a fading of his association of hands with carrots, and the biting disappeared.

When I felt the time was right, when we had dealt with many of his other poor behaviour issues, I decided to try to deal with the big bogey – the trailer! Resistance was high, and the first few times I got the trailer close, it was a bit of a car crash (nearly literally one day). Some evenings I was at a loss to know what to do to start the change. He sweated profusely with fear and foamed at the mouth while rearing and pulling away constantly. I scratched my head, licked my wounds and bruises and read everything I could on horse behaviour. I felt very much 'I'm ok/ you're blooming not' as he reared and crashed around the yard. I also felt myself move into 'I'm not ok/ you are' at times when he dragged me across the concrete on the end of a lead rope as if I weighed nothing at all, and mattered much less! If I became fearful or cross, it never improved anything, and I was just left feeling incapable.

I know when leading teams we can sometimes define ourselves not by the large number of colleagues we have managed successfully towards high performance, but rather by the one difficult colleague who resists, displays defiance or undermines our confidence in some way. A better, truer perspective would be to realise the percentages of success we do have. I like to think I have a good batting average with people and animals (I have trained dogs in the past) and decided I really wanted Polo to reach his potential. I returned to working on the relationship on the ground and learnt about 'join up' and watched numerous horse whisperers at work. I learnt a few new approaches myself and started to implement them.

Gradually I realised that there were occasional times, generally when I felt calmer and more relaxed, that Polo appeared to be changing. He and I seemed to understand each other better and we began to step forward. When there was no agenda or time pressure to get anywhere, there was much better progress. I realised that this was when I remained totally assertive throughout our session. When I was making the way forward very clear, without ambiguity and without force and noticing when he got things right, his behaviour began to change. Step by step we got closer to the trailer without fear or resistance, until finally he did it. 'Catching him doing it right' in exactly the right moment now means I can also lunge him (make him walk round me at a distance) with only spoken instructions to change his gait from walk to trot, and on to the faster canter.

I know he still doesn't particularly like trailers or enclosed spaces, but he trusts me enough to walk onto a small metal contraption which then gets towed along bumpy, noisy roads to a new location, and trusts me to bring him home afterwards. It's a big ask, to be honest, and I understand that. If he takes three attempts to go on (without, I'm glad to say, the rearing and dashing around), I am assertive with him.

Colleagues sometimes have to take on and complete tasks they would rather not, and as managers we need to motivate and continue to ask. I realise this is so similar to how I now feel around the large, sometimes smelly and very strong colleague I have called Polo. I ask clearly and kindly for him to go onto a trailer and he does, even though he would rather not. We have sorted the last bogey, changed his undesirable behaviour to a desirable behaviour, and he is now taking part in occasional shows and may achieve his potential.

If I had been aggressive in trying to get behaviour change, I believe Polo may have become dangerous and ultimately ended his days badly, certainly without reaching his full potential. If I had been passive and allowed his pushy and aggressive behaviour, I believe he would also have ended his days badly, again without the fulfilled life he now has.

He is fit for change, and now if ever he has to move on, he would find a good home as he has no vices, is eminently saleable and a pleasure to be around. Polo likes to go out to new places now, and I use him in my Equine Assisted NLP coaching, where he is incredibly sensitive to clients and their emotions and feelings.

SALLY FOAN, DIRECTOR, PEOPLE TREE TRAINING
WWW.PEOPLETREETRAINING.CO.UK

What a powerful success story. Hopefully it gives you a taster of what can be achieved. If Sally can do that with a big, impressive horse who doesn't speak English, you can do that with your people!

THE TEST

Putting the tools to the test
Try things out
Award winning case study
Gather 360 feedback
1:1 coaching to keep you going
The follow up and call to action

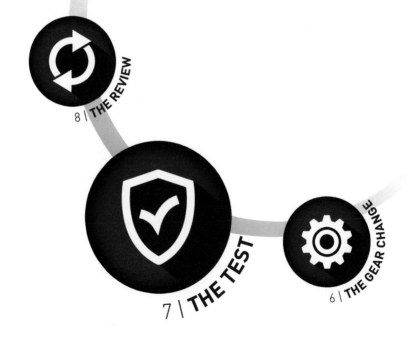

8 | THE REVIEW

7 | THE TEST

6 | THE GEAR CHANGE

THE TEST

Put the tools to the test

The tools you receive as part of the Liberating Leadership programme are amazing. There are some questionnaires to complete, and there are other tools which are an inherent part of the Liberating Leadership book and programme.

The self-assessment questionnaires are:

- *Insights Discovery*® to identify your personal preferences
- *Underlying Beliefs* to check where you are on the High Challenge/High Support scale
- *Process Skills* to see how you use the 15 Skills and 4 Step Process
- *Motivation Inventory* to help you understand your own motivations
- *Situational Consistency* to establish if you are selecting the right *gear* for the situation

As mentioned, the Performance Navigator flowchart is a vital tool now available as an A3 poster with guidelines for anyone who needs it.

The tools embedded in and central to the programme are many, and they all make the leading of people to high performance so much easier. Apart from the elements we have already talked about in The Crux, like Positive Regard and Genuineness, there are many others. There are three I would particularly like to share with you because they are crazily simple yet profound, and I think will be of tremendous use to you right now:

1   The Onion Model

2   The Change Sheet

3   The Flight Plan

Tool 1: The Onion Model

In my experience, leaders can often find it difficult to separate the person from the behaviour. In their mind, when the person does things wrong, the whole person is wrong. This thought provokes an emotional rather than rational response in you, the leader. If you experience an adverse physical response, like your muscles tensing when someone speaks or is near you, then you know the problem is yours. You wonder how as leader you can sort the whole person out, and sometimes you don't even want to try.

Well, you don't have to. You do some work on yourself to develop your Positive Regard for the person by thinking about the last time you felt good about them. Go back to the end of Chapter 2 to check what I did to turn round my thinking about Sam. It is much easier with your children – they have your unconditional love, and it is easy just to comment on their behaviour. We seem to lose this ability as adults in charge of teams and more quickly trash the whole person.

Imagine an onion with its many layers, like a person.

At the very centre of the person is their personality, the very essence of who they are. No-one has a right to interfere with anyone else's personality, and the leader certainly doesn't need to go there.

In the layers around the centre are the person's values, which again can be deep seated and not open to debate – unless you want a black eye! Values and beliefs are things we hold dear, and they have been

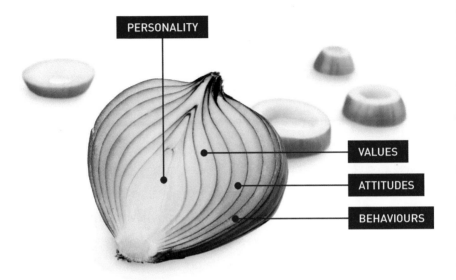

instilled in us since an early age; best not to challenge a person on their religion, or even what football team they support.

In the outer layers of the onion are attitudes and behaviours. Because these are less embedded in who the person is, they are much more open to change, and are the only area the leader rightly can comment on, or indeed can hope to impact on.

This makes things really simple. You don't have to fix the whole person, just ask yourself whether the person's behaviour is consistent right now with achieving your vision. Do they have the right attitude to work?

By working at this level and through feedback, you manage to change their behaviours and improve their attitude to work. They will start to enjoy themselves more. It could have a knock-on effect on their values, and ultimately they may choose to work on their personality with a coach or therapist.

Just remember, if you carefully peel away the outer layers of any onion, everything is fine. And the deeper you cut into it, the more it makes you cry.

Tool 2: The Change Sheet

I have put a Change Sheet at the end of this chapter so you can see it and complete it for any performance issues bothering you right now.

Many leaders will have a million things going round in their head. They have a conversation or one to one with a team member and forget all the things they wanted to say, because it is so very easy to get distracted.

Writing things down is crucial. We forget to write in this world of PCs, phones, tablets and gadgets. Writing things down clears your short term memory of this information and helps process it to long term memory. There is a powerful connection between your hand and your brain. When you write things down it sends a message to your brain that this is important and you mean business. I really urge you to do this.

The Change Sheet is a simple way of writing down your thoughts about a performance issue. What actually is the issue? Write this at the top of the sheet.

Now down the left hand side of the sheet, write what the person is currently doing wrong, the behaviours you want to correct. If you find yourself commenting on their personality in general terms, then bring yourself back and think how this impacts on what they actually do in very specific terms. Instead of saying 'They are really sloppy', write in what way they are sloppy. Is it that they don't stop and check their work, or the way they dress, or the way they respond to customers or file papers? Write down the points as clearly as you can.

Having listed these, in the right hand column you write what the person should be doing in behavioural terms. This gives you the opportunity to view the person behaving at their best. What would they be doing if they were doing the job excellently? Again, make the points really clear. For my son Sam, it was 'Put your washing in the washing basket by 7pm every Friday'. If he was behaving excellently in this respect, that's what he would be doing.

Having written your Change Sheet and captured your thoughts in very clear terms – the general issue, the behaviours currently not up to scratch, and what the person needs to do to improve dramatically – it makes it very easy for you to have a good one to one session with them. There is hope and possibility. You are being explicit, and the person knows what to do to improve. And they know that you believe they can do it.

You keep this under constant review, and if they don't make the changes there needs to be a penalty. There is a whole chapter on this in the *Liberating Leadership* book.

Tool 3: The Flight Plan Analogy

This one is so cool for giving you the confidence to catch people doing something right every day and give them a quick reprimand to put them back on track when they are going off the rails. This is how you maximise performance through feedback.

If you are the pilot in a plane, when you take off from point A, you *always* know where you are going to land (position D). You would never take off without knowing where you are going. We are talking about a trans-Atlantic flight, not playing around in a biplane!

Along the way, you have to check in at various beacons (positions B and C) which don't necessarily follow in a straight line – you are taking the best route for the weather conditions, thermals and other air traffic. It is when planes don't check in at these set beacons that air traffic control knows that something is amiss.

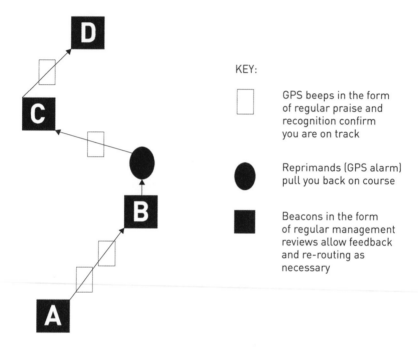

KEY:

☐ GPS beeps in the form of regular praise and recognition confirm you are on track

⬤ Reprimands (GPS alarm) pull you back on course

■ Beacons in the form of regular management reviews allow feedback and re-routing as necessary

Between beacons, the plane is getting constant GPS beeps to let you, the pilot, know you are well on track to the next beacon. In the flight shown, if there was no alarm, or reprimand, after beacon B, the plane would miss the destination by a mile. The alarm is enough to pull the plane back on track, then another GPS beep – you're still on track, thank goodness, and you fly over the next beacon and breathe a sigh of relief. When you land everyone cheers, there is great celebration – you made it!

This flight plan analogy makes the giving of negative feedback much more simple and doable, and the need for giving constant positive feedback so obvious.

These are just some of the tools. There are many more.

Try things out

Once you have all the tools, including completed self-assessment questionnaires, you need to put your new learning to the test.

It is easy if you are just about to take on a team. You can start at the beginning by observing the current climate and analysing the situation accurately, having a visible personal style, and setting your vision and the ground rules. Start the way you mean to go on.

For leaders who have been working with their team for a while, it isn't so clear cut. What I say to them is to draw a line in the sand, define their vision and ground rules, call the team together and make a fresh start. Include the team on the journey. Tell them from now on you'll be giving them feedback every day so they'll know if their actions are consistent with your vision or not. If they can't follow your vision, they are welcome to follow their own...elsewhere, just like in the film *Coach Carter*.

If you understand why you are going through the programme in the first place, you will know what problems you are trying to solve, like how to:

- get people working together instead of in silos
- retain people longer and cut the costly recruitment cycle
- reduce the amount of squabbling and bickering that goes on
- improve sales and productivity
- develop greater team rapport and effectiveness

- drive change
- raise the profile of the team or organisation

You can then measure any improvement across these indicators. The next case study shows how, and the dramatic impact such training can have on bottom line performance.

Award-winning Case Study

In 2008, the then Meningitis Trust needed a dramatic change from the old style command and control culture to a more embracing, collaborative style. The incoming Chief Executive, Sue Davie, grabbed the bull by the horns and started to implement culture change through the 8 Point plan. She described it like this:

'As a support organisation, the Meningitis Trust was very people centred, but mostly externally. Under the previous CEO, the internal people aspect of the organisation had not been a focus, and this resulted in staff turnover of 20% plus (and with recruitment being expensive and very challenging in a rural community, this was a huge issue). Absenteeism and sickness were high, and training was ad hoc, with those who shouted loudest getting the most. Teams were not encouraged to work together, and individuals believed it was up to their manager to develop them.

It was clear we needed to find a way to:

- Enable the organisation to survive – ensuring people were not left to suffer in silence after meningitis
- Enable the organisation to grow in its ability to deliver its vision in an increasingly challenging environment
- Improve effectiveness of the organisation – enabling more to be done with the same or less with strong team working
- Provide an environment where personal development is encouraged and achieved, and instigate effective succession planning

The Trust needed a programme which would fundamentally change the way they worked: a transformational programme which would develop each individual, have an impact on each team and allow the whole organisation to grow. They needed more collaborative working across departments, with a feeling they were working as one team towards a common goal, rather than disparate working groups, each fighting their corner.

The impact of the programme significantly exceeded Sue's aspirations, and strengthened the organisation considerably. The performance improvements they saw were:

- staff turnover halved, absenteeism cut by a third retention at all-time high, with 92% of staff having over 12 months service, compared with 79% in previous three years
- recruitment expenditure dropped from £30k in year before programme to £7k
- media coverage increased by 60%

- the core services were able to support 20% more people than before without any increase in cost
- a major donor programme was established due to increased confidence and knowledge-base in the organisation

The programme was well-received by staff who felt their skills and expertise had improved and their passion ignited. They had a chance to get involved with different projects and some experienced it as life-enhancing.

Sue also commented that, 'You need to see it as a journey which is ongoing. During that journey you need to sit back occasionally and reflect to see what has been achieved and ensure the development continues. It is essential that it lives from the top, and you need to ensure those who naturally take it on board are supported as ambassadors for it, with clear recognition of how they have changed for the good and how they are influencing others as well. As a somewhat reluctant CEO, this programme has personally enabled me to develop confidence I did not know I had and made me a better leader for the Trust.'

These improvements led to the Meningitis Trust and me jointly winning a National Training Award in 2011, and placed the Trust in a position of authority. They then achieved a merger with Meningitis UK. In Oct 2013, together they re-launched as Meningitis Now with Sue at the helm.

Gather 360 feedback

In terms of putting the tools to the test, once the self-assessment questionnaires have been completed, most leaders I train then want to know what others think.

This is a natural and very helpful part of your development as leader. Some people find the thought of gathering feedback about themselves from a range of others very daunting, but we find that those going through the programme ask for it. When we talk about 360 feedback, this means getting all-round feedback from your line manager, your peers, the team members you manage, maybe some clients, suppliers or others you often interact with. You select a range of people, some who know you well and value you, and others who you tend to have more difficulty with.

Their feedback gives you a good view of how others perceive you, and how closely it fits with your self-perception.

With regard to the self-assessment tools I listed at the start of the chapter, the following come with a 360 element:

- *Insights Discovery® Full Circle:* this is a powerful profile for you with feedback from others on what you do well, what you could do better, and general comments about your character and personal preferences.
- *Underlying Beliefs:* there is a line manager and team member version available so they can comment on how well you balance High Challenge and High Support, letting you know where you need to place your development energy.
- *Process Skills:* getting your line manager and team members to tell you how well you do the 15 Skills and operate the 4 Step

Process is incredibly helpful, because others usually have a different view of you than your own.

Why would you want to put yourself through this? Well, because feedback is a gift, as we will see clearly in the next chapter. It is not good or bad, it just is. You need to know what others think so you can adapt your style to enhance your interactions with them and drive performance improvement all round. Feedback encourages you to learn continually and be an even better leader.

Without feedback you are simply working in a void of assumed self-awareness. You may think you know yourself well, but maybe not according to others. It is another way of holding up the mirror for you to see yourself from slightly different angles.

1:1 coaching to keep you going

It's said that training without coaching is just entertainment. I'm not sure who said that, but intuitively it makes sense.

The biggest breakthroughs can happen in a one to one session. This is because you can explore and go deeper than in a group training session. You can be yourself and get help with any limiting beliefs or questions you may not want to share openly in a group, spending longer on the issues you need to discuss.

In early 2013, I started a six month coaching programme with Ali. My needs were to explore where I was with my business, understand my frustrations and decide where my direction should change. My first sessions were soul searching and I felt a bit daunted by the prospect of a meeting a couple of times. Ali guided me to dig deep into my motivations and concerns and we worked through each area of my life and work. After each session, Ali sent on the actions that we had agreed, and I, slowly but surely, started ticking them off. I made some big career decisions during and, interestingly, in the months that followed my coaching, and am still doing so now, with confidence and determination. I know that this would have taken longer, I would have felt more isolated and the resulting actions would not be reaping rewards if I had not had coaching support and challenge.

AMANDA DOWNS, DIRECTOR, COMMERCIAL LEADERSHIP
WWW.COMMERCIALLEADERSHIP.COM

I was delivering a programme in 2011 called *Transactional to Transformational Leadership* commissioned by The Learning Trust in Hackney for school heads and deputies. Initially it was just a three day programme, which was all there was budget for at the time. But the delegates demanded some one-to-one time, or rather two-to-one – the head and deputy together with me, so they could privately get to the root of some issues that were going on at their school. All credit to them, they got it, along with a follow up day. One-to-one time then became an integral part of the programme for future cohorts, and, driven by the people, in essence it became a five day instead of three day programme.

What amazed me was that the heads and deputies needed the programme in the first place when they had access to many leadership training courses commissioned by the National College of School

Leadership. But what they found valuable with this programme was working on real life issues together through the 8 Point Plan. The Plan meant they had a process to follow; they had a route map; they knew where to start and could see where they were every step of the way, rather than having to work it out for themselves from a series of more disjointed modules.

I build in one-to-one time for each of the programmes I deliver for teams of leaders to help embed their learning and understanding, and help to make the changes truly transformational and lasting. I've done this for leaders in the Royal Society of Medicine in London, Sunswept Resorts in St Lucia, and many more.

The leadership programme has certainly enabled the management team to have the confidence and skills to set out more clearly the vision for the department and the expectations of staff and the department – in terms of performance but also of expressions of leadership style and culture. We have built on a number of aspects and have recently run some 'back to basics' sessions with staff who have been empowered to define how things could/should work, standards of performance, etc. We have incorporated aspects of the programme into our annual appraisal system in order to ensure that the learning and development is kept alive. There is more to do, but it has been essential underpinning for the management team.

Be brave! It takes time and courage to recognise that things perhaps need to change/be developed, and this is all the more difficult if you have been working in the area for some time. I would also say don't underestimate the time that it takes – the preparation time, time for training and follow-up. It requires a high level of reflection (individual and organisational) and this can be quite difficult at times. There needs to be buy-in from the senior management team as well as some key opinion formers in the team/department. Organisations also have to remember that investment in staff development rather than solely on the job training is a worthwhile and necessary investment!'

CAROLINE LANGLEY, DIRECTOR, ACADEMIC DEPARTMENT,
ROYAL SOCIETY OF MEDICINE, 2013

The follow up and call to action

We build in some follow up training a few months down the line. By this time, leaders have been trying out the tools, implementing their new vision and ground rules, moving through the steps of the process, mindfully using the skills. By repeating some of the questionnaires we can track progress as well as review all the company-wide indicators, like the Meningitis Trust did.

This leads us into Chapter 8 – the last point in the powerful 8 Point Plan. But first, here is the Liberating Leadership Change Plan for every performance issue.

Liberating Leadership – Change Sheet

Performance Issue:	
Present Undesirable Behaviours (Less of required)	Future Desirable Behaviours (More of required)

THE REVIEW

Reflect and review:
The Learning Cycle
Readjust when necessary
Dealing with dramatic feedback
Apply cruise control

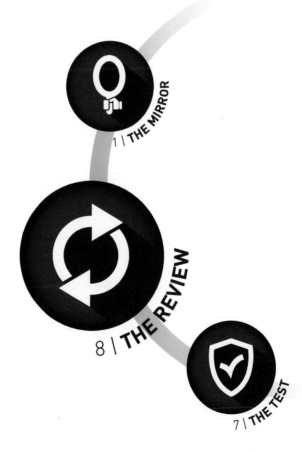

1 | THE MIRROR

8 | THE REVIEW

7 | THE TEST

THE REVIEW

The world is round, and the place which may seem like the end may also be only the beginning.

IVY BAKER PRIEST

Reflect and review

At this point we need to talk about the Learning Cycle, because often important parts of the cycle are missed. This particular cycle is an integral part of the Liberating Leadership programme, and this eighth point of the plan completes the cycle for you.

The way we describe the Learning Cycle is like this:

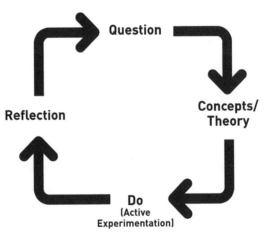

Learning always starts with a question
...and you must complete the cycle

You can do everything but no learning happens unless you reflect... and then start questioning again... "How can I do that better?"

Reflection

Question

Concepts/ Theory

People often get stuck here - they just want to know the theory

Do
(Active Experimentation)

These people don't want the theory, they just want to get on and 'Do'!

- All learning starts with a *Question*. What do I need to know? What is this? Why?
- After the question you start to find the answer through *Research:* you look at concepts and theories to try and make sense of things and find out enough information to get going.
- Then you apply your learning by taking *Action*. You are in the active phase of implementation.
- After that you should go into a period of *Reflection* and review – what went well? What didn't? What can we learn from this? How can we do it better?

For the best learning experience, the cycle needs to be completed. But often, those higher in Fiery Red 'do it now' energy start with the question then jump straight into action, not always stopping to find out what else they might need to know. For them action is better than sitting around talking about it. Then, because time is pressing and there is always so much to do, they often jump straight to the next question.

Others get stuck in the research phase, believing they can't get going until they have all the information – paralysis by analysis. This tendency is found more in those with high Cool Blue 'wanting to get things right' energy, or in people who suffer from a lack of confidence, or with blocks preventing them from taking action. These blocks could be real or perceived.

Mostly, the reflect and review phase is missed out or not visited so frequently – but only by spending time here will you complete the learning cycle. By spending time here, you will always come up with the best next question and start the cycle again.

It is for this exact reason I have built in time for reflection and review in the 8 Point Plan.

Let's assume that you and your managers have been through the plan. You started with a question like 'How can I get my staff to be more motivated and engaged?' You then went into a period of research and deep learning with Insights Discovery® and the Liberating Leadership programme, including a 360 exercise and coaching. Here you were understanding more about yourself; understanding the process of leadership; understanding what others think of you; and understanding what you need to do to improve.

Then you were into a phase of doing – setting your vision, the ground rules, and trying things out with the team. You were putting your learning to the test and resolutely going about building a high performing team. It takes time to get all this going and you needed resilience to see it through; time to take your people with you on a journey from Transactional to Transformational leadership with strength and dignity, passion and compassion.

To complete the cycle, we build in a follow up exercise about nine months on, where we stop and review with you how things are going. It's good to repeat some of the questionnaires at this stage, particularly the Underlying Beliefs questionnaire – the one that maps you on the High Challenge/High Support scale – and Process Skills, to see if things are improving. You can also repeat the 360 exercise and get feedback from others.

With most of our clients, improvements are clearly visible. Team members are much happier and more involved. When this happens to you as leader, you feel a sense of warmth and achievement. You know you are on the right track to achieving a high performing team, or to raising their game further if they are already performing well. There is a level of energy, purpose and commitment that wasn't there before; motivation and engagement are high.

If leaders are not feeling like this, the chances are they have not been rigorously applying the process, focusing on the central mindset or catching people doing something right. Leaders often get so wrapped up in the task and the rush of pressing actions and fire-fighting. They tell me about issues in the team, and I see their *Liberating Leadership* book still sitting on the shelf in pristine condition. It should be looking used and battered like mine. I ask them where they are on the Performance Navigator, which mostly they have forgotten to use.

This is very normal, because often leaders are trying to change years of behaving in a particular way, and really have to focus on new ways of working. It is always difficult when there are so many pressing things to do. This is why it is important to stop and review things, and I can purposefully help people to plan their course of action, get things on track, or even try a different tack.

You will know if you've got it right, because these are the results of high performance leadership:

1   your team is all on task and motivated
2   they are supportive of each other and of you
3   they're energised, engaged, and have upped their game
4   they support your vision and know what to do
5   everyone is consistently performing at their very best

6   the team meets challenges head on, taking everything in their
         stride

7   there's high morale, involvement and commitment

8   they manage change well and cope with stress brilliantly

9   your team is seen as a high performing team of winners

As a result of this review, readjustments may need to be made. You have
a new plan of action and may need to tweak the way you do things. You
are perfectly completing the Learning Cycle...and starting again with the
best question to come next.

Readjust when necessary

The readjustments would be a good thing to look at next. Sometimes it
is uncomfortable having to tweak the way you do things, but unless you
really commit to being the best leader of people and constantly
developing yourself, you are setting yourself and your people up to fail.

Often it is when things are going well that something happens, and
you need to be ready for this. Key people leave for good reasons;
customers change their buying habits; funding streams shift; the world
changes. In organisational development, to stay ahead of the market the
idea is that you start doing the research, scanning the environment and
planning the next period of growth when you are still building the first
phase.

If you wait until the first phase is complete and you are on a roll it is
too late, and you will find there is a decline before you can start building
the next phase. The world has moved on and you can't respond quickly
enough to the changes. It wouldn't take much for you to think of a few

well-known organisations which have failed to keep up with the market, suffered a massive decline and have had to claw their way back. It's hard work and some don't make it.

There are some inspirational leaders out there who are, or were, really good at spotting trends and reinventing themselves – Richard Branson, Steve Jobs, Tony Robbins; or Madonna, Kylie, Lady Gaga, to name but a few. What these fantastic people have in common is that they kept abreast of and responded well to changes in their environment, mood and current thinking. They have changed their look, their style, rebranded, branched out, while very much keeping the essence of who they are.

The same needs to happen for you to keep developing as a leader to stay ahead of the game. Now all this work is underway, it might be a good time to hold up the mirror again and see how you're doing.

> *Your vision becomes clear when you look inside your heart. Who looks outside, dreams. Who looks inside, awakens.*
>
> **DR CARL JUNG**

Dealing with 'dramatic' feedback

Here is a beautiful story to illustrate the need to look inside, or indeed look in the mirror, from my friend and colleague Lisa Brice, Trainer of NLP, executive coach and business consultant. It reminds us that feedback is indeed a gift, and this is what she wrote in a memorable newsletter:

'You Are Not Constant... '

The words stood out like they were highlighted in red, and I didn't really hear the rest of the sentence: 'You are not constant... '

Well it definitely provoked a response within, and I was quite proud of myself for not verbalising my internal reaction in the moment. Luckily the circumstances were such that exploring the comment was inappropriate there and then, and it wasn't until the next day after a great night's sleep that I had the opportunity to explore my thoughts about the feedback.

I was really curious about where my thinking went and the questions I asked myself:

- Is that just his experience of me, or is it how other people experience me too?
- Not being constant doesn't match with my experience of myself – I believe I am constant in the matters that count: friendships, business agreements, delivering on my promises. I am dependable!
- The fact I reacted to the feedback means that it is worth exploring.
- Interesting that the feedback was given as an identity statement: "You are ..."
- Is it true that I am not constant or is it true that at times my behaviour is not constant?
- How am I not constant? Could my desire to be flexible be perceived as not being constant?

I find it fascinating how often, especially in a business context, I hear people giving feedback at an identity level: you are a bad communicator; you are a poor manager; you are a great leader; you are a bad customer service adviser. What is the point of that feedback? How can the other person use it? It is only their opinion yet they have delivered it as universal truth.

So this is Lisa, a professional at the top of her game, still taking time out to reflect.

How would you respond to feedback like this, directed at the centre of the onion, commenting on your essence as a human being rather than what you are doing?

We quite often want to justify ourselves, argue or immediately refute the accusation. If any feedback upsets us, causes us to react angrily, causes us some anxiety, or causes a physical reaction in us, like our body stiffening or feeling slightly sick, we know it is the perfect cue to do some work on ourselves.

Responding to the statement, 'You are not constant' with internal enquiry, like Lisa did, takes skill, but you can do it. Say thank you for the gift, and work out the cause of your distress. You'll see how everything is connected, because we are now back with that secret skill of Explicitness.

Lisa goes on to say:

Would it not be more useful and supportive for the person to describe the behaviours that led them to come up with their summary statement 'You are a bad communicator'? Perhaps, for instance, 'When you raised your voice and invaded Mary's personal space on Tuesday afternoon in the sales office, I noticed that Mary turned bright red, lowered her eye contact and whispered her responses to your questions. What do you think was the impact on Mary of your communication? What was your purpose for your conversation with Mary? Did you achieve that? What could you do differently next time?"

Developmental feedback in my opinion is best given at a behavioural level, thus allowing the person to choose a different behaviour if they're not getting the result they want. Changing one's identity in my experience is a longer term project and not so easily done; changing ones behaviour is just a matter of choice. When I am giving appreciative feedback, I sometimes like to 'talent spot' at an identity level: you are an amazing person, you are a great sales person, you are an inspirational leader. While it doesn't provide the receiver with a lot of information, it is often aspirational.

LISA BRICE, FOUNDER OF CHOOSE2B AND HORSES FOR COURSES

HTTP://WWW.LISABRICE.CO.UK

Remember: **Lead Explicitly And Deliver Excellent Results.**

Apply cruise control

Take heart: in terms of continually developing, sometimes all that is needed is a tweak rather than a major overhaul. Going back to the car driving analogy, you know that an oil change or realigning the tracking might be all that's needed to keep things in tip top condition for MOT. Actually, if we paid as much attention to developing our leadership style as we do to maintaining our cars, the difference would be phenomenal – and with this amount of consideration we would definitely run for longer and more smoothly.

You know when you first start riding a bicycle or driving a car, you tend to exaggerate your actions and over-correct if you are going off course. The ride is jerky as you swerve from side to side, or take a corner too wide, or swerve too far out as you go round a parked car.

The more you practise the easier it gets, and the more skilled you get. And when you have put all that work into developing your team, Derek, who is a sailor, would say, 'A gentle tap on the tiller is often all that's needed to keep the boat on track'.

With the 8 Point Plan you now have a great way of getting your boat on track in the first place, then gently keeping it there while you scan the horizon to see what else is going on in the sea around you.

While we are on the subject of boats and sea, it's worth mentioning waves. Here is a little taster from the last chapter in Derek's *Liberating Leadership* book:

The future…is not as predictable as it once seemed to be. The only certainty is there will be further waves of change, just as the sea waves roll in from beyond the horizon, some gentle, others threatening, with the occasional unpredictable rogue wave, larger and more devastating than the rest. Some organisations and individuals within them have 'surfed' such waves of change well, while others have bobbed about in the backwash like jetsam. Still others, denying the existence of such waves, turned their back to them, only to receive a cold, sharp shock when a wave, larger than the rest, caught them unawares.

DR DEREK BIDDLE, LIBERATING LEADERSHIP

I hope you've found the journey through this book enlightening and a support to your development as an exceptional, dignified leader and developer of people.

What is the first action you need to take?

When is the best time to start?

Best wishes, and enjoy the journey to increased profits and more productive, happier people.

Liberating
Leadership | LEADING & DEVELOPING HIGH PERFORMANCE

by Dr Derek Biddle & Ali Stewart

The *Liberating Leadership* book forms the bedrock of our dynamic training programme. It takes leaders on a path from Transactional to Transformational leadership, leaving nothing to chance.

There's one thing that's certain, regardless of your business type and size: if you want to grow your business, it means leading and managing your people. The more effectively you lead, the better your team will perform and the more profitable your business will be.

Imagine... you are a leader. You take your team to the top of a skyscraper and out onto the roof. The roof is flat, there are no barriers round the edge of the roof, it is dark...and the team members have roller skates on. You ask them to skate around, but they huddle together in the middle, not daring to go far. It is very scary for them.

But now, if you floodlight the roof with your vision, which is so bright the team can't fail to see where they are going, and put strong railings round the edge (the clear boundaries you impose), then the team will skate to the edges, using all the space available. They know they are safe. They can try out new moves, knowing you'll catch them if they fall. They will put on a magnificent display, exceeding all your expectations.

To achieve this clarity of purpose, to shine the light authentically and set the boundaries, a leader needs specific skills. Anyone can learn them. You don't need exceptional characteristics, a high IQ or a degree in human resources.

This book leads you through the process, helping you become a truly liberated leader of people.

> *Leadership is lifting a person's vision to higher sights; the raising of a person's performance to a higher standard; the building of a personality beyond its normal limitations.*

PETER F DRUCKER

Follow us on Facebook to keep abreast of developments.

https://www.facebook.com/AliStewartandCo

Pioneering
Professional | SELF DIRECTING
SKILLS FOR LIFE

by Dr Derek Biddle & Ali Stewart

This is a powerful little book based on research into what make high fliers fly!

These high fliers are the ones who become successful very quickly while still having a great life outside work. Noticeably others who work very hard seem to struggle to accomplish the same kind of results.

The key is to understand the underlying mindset of these highly successful people, and the 7 Key Skills they employ.

Success isn't down to having a high IQ, it is more do with high Emotional Intelligence. The 7 Key Skills include managing your workload without becoming swamped; negotiating for success; managing other people well; shaping your own environment; presenting solutions not problems; and effectively planning your own career.

This book is great if you feel that you are stuck in a rut with deadlines and opportunities being missed. You can learn how to manage your manager with ease, and understand the common time wasters that will catch you out time and again.

It gives you the opportunity to review and enhance your thinking and skills, raise your game, enjoy your career and lift your performance to a whole new level.

The book is available from our website, Amazon and Kindle:
http://alistewartandco.com/our-services/pioneering-professional/
And do ask us for information on the supporting coaching and training.

NEXT STEPS

If you have read this far, I know you are looking for something – at the very least some help and support.

Maybe as a leader you need someone to walk with you through the steps you know you need to take. It can be lonely at the top, and sharing the journey with others makes it so much easier, more enjoyable and exciting. It will expand your thinking and set you on track to greater success in developing a dream team of super-engaged motivated people.

Maybe you are a coach, trainer or consultant wanting to leverage greater sales and have the benefit of a robust leadership programme to offer to clients; a programme you can brand as your own, with books in your own colours; a professional award-winning programme with excellent resources to raise your game dramatically.

Insights into Liberating Leadership – One Day Accelerator

For anyone interested in developing their skill as a powerful leader of people:

- See the 8 Point Plan in real life.
- Experience resources to build your skill and inspire action.
- Delight in the success of others who have experienced dramatic performance improvements using the plan.

Liberating Leadership Programme for Leaders – Eight Week Programme

For any business owner, leader or entrepreneur needing a grounded, powerful process for developing their people:

- We run in-house or open programmes – tell us what you need.
- Develop the mindset of the highest performing leaders of people.
- Resolutely learn the process and build the vital skills needed to make the most astounding improvements in your people.

Liberating Leadership Accreditation for Facilitators – Three Day Intensive

For any coaches, trainers or consultants wanting to build their skill and product offering for leaders and teams, and raise their standing:

- Experience the programme as a delegate to build your leadership muscle.
- Work with the powerful resources available and appreciate their impact.
- Decide the level you want to play at in terms of branding your own material and accessing all the resources. There's a model for everyone.

For accredited practitioners there is a Mastermind Group. We meet throughout the year, and there are private forums on Facebook and LinkedIn. We really look forward to welcoming you to the group.

Contact Ali for a chat: http://alistewartandco.com/contact/

ABOUT THE AUTHOR – ALI STEWART

Ali started Ali Stewart & Co, coaching you to achieve and grow, in July 2004, and hasn't looked back.

Having co-authored the *Liberating Leadership* and *Pioneering Professional* books and established the accrediting body in 2008, she has trained over 500 leaders and accredited over sixty practitioners to deliver the programmes with outstanding success. She is looking to grow this body of people so that other trainers, coaches and consultants have access to this powerful model to help them grow their own and their clients' businesses.

As she is so passionately moved by the Insights Discovery® model, Ali is also a Regional Mentor for all UK Insights® licensed practitioners. In 2012 she was one of the first practitioners in the world to be accredited in the Insights® Deeper Discovery model.

The *Pioneering Professional* is the perfect programme for any organisation, especially if they are training their leaders. If in tandem they train their staff to be more pioneering and self-directing, it's less of an uphill struggle. Together leaders and staff excel. It is also a brilliant book for professionals with no line-management responsibility.

Ali's business has been built with her amazing team, based on the ethos of Liberating Leadership. Her whole purpose is to help leaders to lead with strength and dignity and individuals to find their best life with passion and compassion.